GREATER EXPECTATIONS

The challenge of the Sermon on the Mount

by Ray Markham

GREATER EXPECTATIONS

The challenge of the Sermon on the Mount

by Ray Markham

Contents

Preface — 5

Chapter one
Characteristic Characteristics
Matthew 5:3-12 — 7

Chapter two
Sprinkled and Shining
Matthew 5:13-16; 6:22, 23 — 44

Chapter three
But I Tell You . . .
Matthew 5:17-48 — 63

Chapter four
Don't Be Like Them
Matthew 6:1-18 — 117

Chapter five
Dos and Don'ts
Matthew 6:19-7:6 — 139

Chapter six
Four Twos
Matthew 7:7-29 — 166

Dedication

To my wife Sheila, and my mother Dora, in appreciation of their unfailing love, support and prayers.

Please note:
All Bible quotations are from the
New International Version
unless otherwise stated.

Abbreviations:

GNB – Good News Bible
KJV – King James Version (Authorised Version)
LB – Living Bible
NIV – New International Version
JBP – J. B. Phillips
TEV – Today's English Version

Copyright © 2002 by Ray Markham

First published in 2002

All rights reserved. No part of this publication
may be reproduced
in any form without prior
permission from the publisher.

British Library Cataloguing in Publication Data.
A catalogue record for this book is available
from the British Library.

ISBN 1-903921-01-5

Published by
AUTUMN HOUSE
Alma Park, Grantham, Lincs, England, NG31 9SL

2 4 6 8 10 9 7 5 3 1

Preface

The teachings of Jesus are the most important ever given to mankind, and it is essential that we both understand and apply them to our everyday lives. This book examines those teachings given on the Sermon on the Mount and attempts to provide an analysis of them which is both thorough and thought-provoking.

When writing this book, I had two particular aims in mind. Firstly, to explain what Jesus taught, clearly, concisely and cogently, in a style that is easy to read and understand. Secondly, to apply these teachings in practical ways to everyday life.

This book provides the basic points to be drawn from Jesus' teaching, for the benefit of Christians who are young in the faith, and also a great deal of material for the more mature Christian to reflect on, including many references for further study.

I also had in mind the needs of group leaders who are looking for a book which will help them to prepare studies on the Sermon on the Mount or guide the group through the teaching it contains. That is why, at the end of each chapter, there is a carefully prepared set of questions designed to promote discussion about, and encourage the application of, the teaching in that section. The group leader can either select from the comprehensive list provided, or use them all over a number of sessions. The questions can also be used to aid personal study and reflection.

If readers find that this book helps them to understand the teachings of Jesus contained in the Sermon on the Mount, while at the same time enabling them to see how they can be put into practice, then I shall be delighted to have succeeded in what I set out to do.

Ray Markham

CHAPTER 1

Characteristic Characteristics

Matthew 5:3-12

The world in which we live has certain expectations of us as members of society. God has far greater expectations of us as members of His kingdom. In the Sermon on the Mount, Jesus talks about the characteristics, attitudes and lifestyle which God expects to see in the lives of all those who are His followers.

Count, consider, commit

The content of this Sermon is not directed so much at the crowd in general, but rather at His disciples (5:1-2): those who have committed themselves to following Him.

Jesus did not intend these teachings to apply just to the disciples of His day, but to all those who would choose to follow Him down the centuries. On other occasions, Jesus made it quite clear that being a disciple was not something to be entered into lightly, because there was a cost to be counted (Matthew 8:18-22; 16:24; Mark 8:34; Luke 9:23, 57-62; 14:26-35). Much thought and consideration need to be given before taking the decision to commit oneself to discipleship.

To emphasise these points, Jesus gave two examples: one about a man who wants to build a tower; the other about a king who is about to go to war with another king (Luke 14:28-32). Before deciding to construct his tower, the builder would first sit down and estimate the cost of his project to see if he could afford to commit himself to it. If he began and found he could not finish it, he would be ridiculed by everyone who saw the evidence of his folly. Indeed, there are many so-called 'follies' one can visit today: building projects that were left unfinished because the funds ran out. Similarly, the king would sit down and consider whether going to war was a good idea when he was outnumbered two to one.

Jesus wants to make sure that we count the cost and consider the consequences before we commit ourselves to becoming His disciples. Such a decision has far-reaching implications for what should characterise our lives from that point on.

Jesus calls us to be different *from* the world, so that we might make a difference *to* the world.

The Beatitudes

Introduction

In this chapter we are looking at those characteristics which Jesus outlines in what are called 'The Beatitudes' (5:3-12). God expects to see evidence of all of them in our lives. They should be characteristic of all members of His kingdom.

The term 'beatitude' comes from a Latin word *'beatitudo'* meaning 'blessedness'. There are several beatitudes in The Old

Testament, particularly in the Book of Psalms (1:1, 2; 32:1, 2; 41:1; 65:4). The gospels contain various beatitudes given by Jesus (Matthew 11:6; 13:16; 16:17; John 13:17; 20:29), but the phrase is used most frequently to refer to the collection that appears in Matthew 5:3-12.

It is important to realise that neither Jesus nor Matthew called this listing 'The Beatitudes', as neither of them used Latin. It was probably added by scholars who in future years translated the New Testament into Latin from the Greek in which it was written.

All beatitudes begin with the word 'Blessed', sometimes translated as 'Happy'. But neither of these words really captures the full meaning of the original Greek word *makarios* which Matthew uses. The flavour of the word is more a congratulation to those who are already showing this characteristic in their lives, and a recommendation to others to do so, for thereby lies the way of a truly happy and fulfilled life, with rewards that affect our spiritual experience and relationship with God.

✱ Poor in spirit

The first characteristic is that of being 'poor in spirit' (3). This means that we acknowledge that we are sinners who deserve God's wrath and judgement, and throw ourselves on His mercy. We realise that we can do nothing of ourselves to merit acceptance into the Kingdom of Heaven. As the hymn-writer A. M. Toplady put it:

> 'Nothing in my hand I bring,
> Simply to Thy cross I cling;
> Naked, come to Thee for dress;
> Helpless, come to Thee for grace;

Foul, I to the fountain fly;
Wash me, Saviour, or I die.'

Jesus told a parable about a Pharisee and a tax collector who went to the temple to pray (Luke 18:9-14). The tax collector cried out: 'God, have mercy on me, a sinner.' This is the language of someone who was poor in spirit, and his prayer was answered. The Pharisee, on the other hand, was proud in spirit. This was reflected in his prayer, which met with the appropriate response.

John Calvin wrote: 'He only who is reduced to nothing in himself, and relies on the mercy of God, is poor in spirit.' It is only as we adopt this attitude, realising that our salvation is a gift of God and not something we can earn, that we can become members of the Kingdom of Heaven. And God expects us to continue in this attitude so that we may accomplish great things for Him. As C. H. Spurgeon said: 'The way to rise in the kingdom is to sink in ourselves.' What a contrast this is to the society in which we live, where personal pride, independence and self-reliance are all encouraged and praised. The way to rise in the kingdoms of this world is to rise in ourselves.

The prophet Isaiah said: 'For this is what the high and lofty One says – He who lives forever, whose name is holy: "I live in a high and holy place, but also with him who is contrite and lowly in spirit"' (Isaiah 57:15a). Being lowly and poor in spirit before God is where we all need to start, and where we all need to remain. Notice how Isaiah links this with being contrite, which brings us to the next beatitude.

✷ Mourning
The second characteristic is that of mourning (4). While we can

understand why Jesus describes those who are poor in spirit as *makarios*, how could those who mourn possibly come into this category? It is important to understand that here Jesus is not talking about mourning the death of a loved one, but mourning over the sins we have committed. This is what is meant by having a contrite heart. To repent of our sin and ask God's forgiveness is one thing: to weep over the sins we have committed and the grief we have caused our Father God as a result is quite another. As the Holy Communion service section of the 1662 *Prayer Book* puts it: 'We acknowledge *and bewail* [emphasis mine] our manifold sins and wickedness.'

References to this can be found in the Bible. For example, when the priest Ezra was praying and confessing his sins, he was seen to be 'weeping and throwing himself down before the house of God.' (Ezra 10:1). Writing to the church in Corinth concerning the sins they were committing, the apostle Paul said: 'And you are proud! Shouldn't you rather have been filled with grief . . . ?' (1 Corinthians 5:2). They were neither poor in spirit nor contrite in heart. There is a danger that while revelling in the wonder of God's amazing grace, we neglect to mourn and weep for our sinfulness. Speaking through the prophet Isaiah, God says: '"This is the one I esteem: he who is humble and contrite in spirit"' (Isaiah 66:2). The first two characteristics should be inextricably linked.

They certainly were in the case of King David as he repented of his adultery with Bathsheba (2 Samuel 11, 12). In his prayer of repentance, he wrote: 'Have mercy on me, O God, . . . Wash away all my iniquity and cleanse me from my sin. For I know my transgressions, and my sin is always before me. . . . You do not delight in sacrifice, or I would bring it, . . . The sacrifices of God are a broken spirit; a broken and contrite heart, O God, you will not despise' (Psalm 51:1-3,16, 17).

Streams of tears

God expects us to show such contrition, and promises that we 'will be comforted' (5:4). In the Old Testament, bringing comfort and consolation is seen as being one of the ministries of the Messiah who was to come: 'He has sent me to bind up the brokenhearted, . . . to comfort all who mourn' (Isaiah 61:1, 2). Jesus confirmed that He was indeed the One who had come to do this (Luke 4:21). He paid the greatest price so that we might know the greatest comfort any of us can know: that of sins forgiven (Luke 22:19, 20; 1 John 1:7-9).

Sadly, we live in a world where most people do not mourn for their sin. Indeed, in the western world there no longer seems to be any sense of sin. It has become a taboo word, along with 'guilt' and 'shame'. We are encouraged not to feel guilt or shame any more, because these are apparently negative and destructive feelings which repress our natural urges and appetites. The whole concept of sin has been rejected as an outmoded and rather quaint idea, no longer relevant in a modern society where man is his own master, even his own god. The prevailing philosophy seems to be, 'If it feels good, do it'. There is no longer a commonly held, absolute moral code: we make it up as we go along, and what is true for today may not be true for tomorrow. Provided we can justify our actions to ourselves, then that makes them acceptable, and who is to judge us?

The dire consequences of such thinking are to be seen all around us. Our television screens and newspapers are full of examples of it. But how do we react when we see it all? Another aspect of mourning is that we should weep over the evil in the world, and bring it before God in tears of grief. God expects us to cultivate the attitude of the Psalmist who said: 'Streams of tears flow from my eyes, for your law is not obeyed' (Psalm 119:136).

Our comfort is that, no matter how desperate things may seem, God is still in control, and will one day return. And then '"He will wipe every tear from their eyes. There will be no more death or mourning or crying or pain, for the old order of things has passed away." He who was seated on the throne said: "I am making everything new!"' (Revelation 21:4, 5).

✱ Meek

The third characteristic is that of being 'meek' (5). The Greek word *praotes*, which is translated 'meek', means 'gentle', 'humble', 'considerate'. The New English Bible renders it 'those of a gentle spirit'. The apostle Paul urges us to 'Be completely humble and gentle' (Ephesians 4:2), and to 'pursue . . . gentleness' (1 Timothy 6:11). The Authorised Version renders it 'follow after . . . meekness'. Paul also refers to 'the meekness and gentleness of Christ' (2 Corinthians 10:1). Indeed, Jesus speaks of Himself as being 'meek and lowly in heart' (Matthew 11:29, KJV).

'Blessed are the meek' is not a sentence that would be endorsed by the world in which we live. Here, it is more a case of 'Blessed are the strong, the assertive, the dominant'. They are the ones who have the power. The meek just get ignored or trampled on. So how can they possibly 'inherit the earth' ? To understand this, we need to set this sentence against the background of Psalm 37, which Jesus seems to have been quoting from: 'Do not fret because of evil men or be envious of those who do wrong; . . . A little while, and the wicked will be no more; . . . But the meek will inherit the land and enjoy great peace. . . . those the Lord blesses will inherit the land ... Wait for the Lord and keep his way. He will exalt you to inherit the land, . . . when the wicked are cut off, you will see it' (Psalm 37:1, 10, 11, 22, 34).

There is a principle here which operates now and in the future: although the powerful may think they possess the world, they don't; God does. It belongs to Him: and as His children, it therefore belongs to us, the meek of this world. As the apostle Paul puts it: 'Now if we are children, then we are heirs — heirs of God and co-heirs with Christ' (Romans 8:17). The fullness of this inheritance will be realised only in the future, when there will be a new heaven and a new earth for the meek to inherit (2 Peter 3:13; Revelation 21:1).

Meekness personified

There is another aspect to the word 'meek' in the Greek language. It is used to describe an animal that has been trained by its master. It is now disciplined rather than wild; teachable rather than self-willed. It has become meek. Whereas before it was of no use to its master, now it is of great use to him, and its full potential can begin to be realised. This reminds us that not only does God expect us to be gentle and humble, but to be disciplined and teachable, otherwise we are of little use to Him. God can only begin to unlock the potential that we have for Him when we show meekness of spirit before Him. Under the control of God, meekness is strength, and gentleness is power.

Jesus is meekness personified. According to the prophets, it was a characteristic that would mark out the Messiah when He came. In his account of Jesus' entry into Jerusalem to the acclaim of the vast crowds who welcomed Him as their King and Messiah, Matthew reminds us of the prophecy of Zechariah: '"See your king comes to you, gentle [meek – KJV] and riding on a donkey, on a colt, the foal of a donkey"' (Matthew 21:5; see Zechariah 9:9). Interestingly, that colt had never been ridden before, and was therefore not broken in (Mark 11:2; Luke 19:30). Yet as soon as Jesus sat on it, it became meek. What a moving picture this is of the meek colt carrying the meek king towards His meek death (Isaiah 53:7). Was ever a king so meek: yet never did a king have such power!

Meekness, not weakness

There is a third aspect of the word 'meek'. *Praotes* has also been defined as 'the mean between excessive anger and extreme apathy, the quality of the person who is always angry at the right time and never at the wrong time'. Having entered Jerusalem, Jesus is about to demonstrate this for us, and to show us once and for all that meekness is not weakness, as many people seem to think. Indeed, one has to be strong to be meek.

It is interesting that this is Jesus' first act after His being acclaimed publicly as the Messiah for the first time. Matthew describes what happened: 'Jesus entered the temple area and drove out all who were buying and selling there. He overturned the tables of the money-changers and the benches of those selling doves. "It is written," he said to them, " 'My house will be called a house of prayer,' " but you are making it a 'den of robbers' " ' (Matthew 21:12, 13).

Jesus' anger was aroused by the sacrilege of what He saw before Him. In the outer court of the temple, called the 'Court of the Gentiles', was a market for the sale to pilgrims of animals and birds, such as doves, for sacrifice. These creatures were guaranteed to meet all the requirements of the Law of Moses, and were therefore very costly. They had to be paid for with special temple money, and not in the Roman coins in general everyday use. The rate of exchange set by the money-changers was very high. So pilgrims were being cheated not once, but twice: firstly by the money-changers, and secondly by the traders who sold the animals. No wonder Jesus called it 'a den of robbers'. The temple was intended to be a place where all nations of the world could come to worship and pray, and the money-changers and traders were taking advantage of the pilgrims. What a dramatic scene it must have been as chairs and tables, money bowls and their contents, paperwork and writing implements all went flying off in different directions as Jesus strode through the court, with the people scattering to the left and to the right.

There are some important lessons for us here. First of all, being meek doesn't mean that we keep quiet about anything we see that is wrong: it means just the opposite. Wherever there are things going on that are contrary to the teachings of the Bible, God expects us to be prepared to protest and to take appropriate action to fight against them together as His people. Too often we seem to allow our views to be ignored or trampled on. Secondly, we need to do this in a controlled and dignified manner as befits followers of Jesus. He was angry all right that day in the temple, but I can't for one moment imagine Jesus getting out of control or losing His dignity, even in the midst of the mayhem. And it is important for us to remember to be meek at all times and in all places.

✶ Righteous

The fourth characteristic is that of being hungry and thirsty for righteousness (6). While the world around us is hungry and thirsty for wealth and possessions, God expects us, as disciples of Christ and members of His Kingdom, to develop an insatiable appetite for righteousness. While others enthusiastically pursue that which is material, we are to hunger and thirst after that which is spiritual with even greater fervour.

Aspects of righteousness

Righteousness simply means that which is right in God's sight. There are three main aspects to it. The first one concerns our relationship with God. The apostle Paul explains how we have been made righteous in God's sight: 'This righteousness from God comes through faith in Jesus Christ to all who believe' (Romans 3:22). When we repent of our sin and ask God's forgiveness, our relationship with God is restored. Our deepest desire should be for that relationship to be preserved, treasured and developed on a daily basis, with a growing hunger and thirst for more of God. The Psalmist showed such an appetite when he said: 'As the deer pants for streams of water, so my soul pants for you, O God. My soul thirsts for God, for the living God' (Psalm 42:1, 2).

The second aspect concerns our behaviour and conduct. As the apostle Paul puts it: 'Be careful to do what is right in the eyes of everybody' (Romans 12:17). Being righteous in the way we live should be as important to us as eating and drinking are. The Jews paid lip-service to a set of rules just to look good and to win compliments. God does not expect to find such pretence in our lives, but rather an appetite to do what is right in His sight which stems from our hearts, and whose motive is to gain His pleasure, not human plaudits.

Thirdly, we should hunger and thirst for righteousness in the society in which we live. This means being concerned about all practices which are displeasing to God. And such concern should express itself in action against the evils of the day. Martin Luther addressed this issue in his usual forthright manner: 'The command to you is not to crawl into a corner . . . but to run out . . . and to offer your hands and your feet and your whole body, and to wager everything you have and can do.' He went on to explain that what is required of us is '. . . a hunger and thirst for righteousness that can never be curbed or stopped or sated, one that looks for nothing and cares for nothing except the accomplishment and maintenance of the right, despising everything that hinders this end. If you cannot make the world completely pious, then do what you can.'

Promises and parallels

The promise in this verse is that '. . . those who hunger and thirst for righteousness . . . will be filled.' This reflects other promises made in Scripture to those with an appetite. For example: 'He satisfies the thirsty and fills the hungry with good things' (Psalm 107:9), a verse which Mary might have had in mind when she said 'He has filled the hungry with good things' (Luke 1:53). Doing what is right in God's sight is a very satisfying experience.

However, physical hunger is satisfied for a while, but then recurs. There is a spiritual parallel here too. In response to our righteousness, God fills us with His blessings. And the effect of this should be threefold: to make us hungry for an even deeper relationship with Him in our walk together; to make us hungry for an even deeper commitment to Him that is evident in our lifestyles; to make us hungry for an even deeper involvement with Him in tackling social issues.

Just as an appetite for food and drink is essential for physical growth, so an appetite for righteousness is essential for spiritual growth. There is no doubt that we have an appetite for food and drink. The challenge to us is whether we have such an undoubted appetite for righteousness. Little or no spiritual growth usually indicates a lack of such an appetite. Or could it be that we are fostering the wrong kind of appetite, and have allowed the world around us to 'squeeze' us 'into its mould'? (Romans 12:2, J. B. Phillips.)

✶ Merciful

The fifth characteristic is that of being merciful (7). The dictionary defines 'mercy' as 'compassion or forbearance shown to enemies or offenders in one's power'. In other words, we are being merciful when we are in a position to harm someone, or to punish him for something he has done wrong, but we refrain from doing so.

Since Jesus does not give us a list itemising those to whom we should show such mercy, He clearly expects us to show mercy to everyone, just as God does. In Luke's record of this sermon, Jesus says: '"Be merciful, just as your Father is merciful"' (Luke 6:36). Indeed, the subject of mercy crops up on several occasions during Jesus' ministry. The Jews already knew that God required them to show mercy, because the prophet Micah had made this quite clear to them: 'He has showed you, O man, what is good. And what does the Lord require of you? To . . . love mercy' (Micah 6:8). Jesus spoke strongly to the teachers of the law and the Pharisees about it, saying, '"Woe to you, teachers of the law and Pharisees, you hypocrites! You give a tenth of your spices . . . . But you have neglected the more important matters of the law – justice, mercy and faithfulness. You should have practised the latter, without neglecting the former"' (Matthew 23:23). He told them to '"go and learn what this means: 'I desire mercy, not sacrifice'"' (Matthew 9:13). In the parable of the Good Samaritan, we are told to emulate the one who had mercy (Luke 10:37).

This is in complete contrast to the world around us, where being merciful is often perceived as a sign of weakness. Exacting revenge is a much more attractive proposition. On the occasions when mercy is shown, it is usually done with the ulterior motive of getting an advantage out of it for oneself. For example, kidnappers may show mercy by releasing their hostages in order to gain more favourable press coverage for their cause. To its shame, the Church down the years has often shown itself to be no better at being merciful than the world around it.

Hand in hand

In this beatitude, Jesus promises that those who are merciful 'will be shown mercy'. The consequence of failing to show mercy is spelt out for us by James: 'judgement without mercy will be shown to anyone who has not been merciful' (James 2:13). However, we cannot merit God's mercy by being merciful ourselves. We must repent before we can receive God's mercy. And we cannot claim to have truly repented of our sins if we do not show mercy to those who sin against us. This is why the servant in the parable is condemned (Matthew 18:23-35). Having received mercy at the hand of the king, he is expected to show mercy to others, but he doesn't. So the king withdraws his original act of mercy. Receiving mercy and showing mercy go hand in hand.

But we should not show mercy to others just because we feel

we have to, knowing that we won't receive God's mercy if we fail to be merciful. Such a grudging and selfish spirit is unacceptable to God, and does not indicate true repentance. Rather, in the words of the prophet Micah quoted earlier, God expects us to '*love* mercy' [emphasis mine]. Being merciful should be an act of love. We should love it when the opportunity to be merciful presents itself, just as God loves to be merciful to us. As Albert Barnes said: 'Nowhere do we imitate God more than in showing mercy.'

How wonderful it is to know that we come before a God who is 'rich in mercy' and is 'full of compassion and mercy' (Ephesians 2:4; James 5:11). God is in a position to punish us for our sins, and we deserve the punishment: but instead He shows us mercy. As the apostle Paul puts it: 'He saved us . . . because of his mercy' (Titus 3:5), and we have become 'objects of his mercy' (Romans 9:23). Whenever we come to God in repentance, His mercy is assured. In the words of the prophet Isaiah: 'Let the wicked forsake his way and the evil man his thoughts. Let him turn to the Lord, and he will have mercy on him, and to our God, for he will freely pardon' (Isaiah 55:7). We have no claim on God's mercy; we have done nothing to deserve it. May our response to God's abundant gift of mercy be that of the hymn-writer Joseph Addison:

'When all thy mercies, O my God, my rising soul surveys,
Transported with the view, I'm lost in wonder, love and praise.'

✽ Pure in heart
The sixth characteristic is that of being 'pure in heart' (8). Whenever this phrase is used in Scripture it refers to inward purity: in other words, a heart and life that have been cleansed of all sin and defilement. King David prayed to God: 'Create in

me a pure heart' (Psalm 51:10), and spoke of the 'pure heart' that is required in order to enter into God's presence (Psalm 24:4a).

Inward, not outward

By the time of Jesus, the Jewish religious leaders, especially the Pharisees, had become obsessed with outward purity. This was expressed by means of fastidious washing of the body, which they believed made them pure, and therefore fit to take part in all the religious ceremony and ritual. Jesus took them to task about this fixation, showing up their external purity for the sham and hypocrisy that it was. Jesus didn't mince His words when He spoke to them on this subject: '"Woe to you, teachers of the law and Pharisees, you hypocrites! You clean the outside of the cup and dish, but inside they are full of greed and self-indulgence. Blind Pharisee! First clean the inside of the cup and dish, and then the outside also will be clean. Woe to you, teachers of the law and Pharisees, you hypocrites! You are like whitewashed tombs, which look beautiful on the outside but on the inside are full of dead men's bones and everything unclean. In the same way, on the outside you appear to people as righteous but on the inside you are full of hypocrisy and wickedness' (Matthew 23:25-28).

Jesus is telling them in no uncertain terms that what matters to God is inward purity of heart, not outward purity of body. This beatitude emphasises the point, and cuts right across what the Pharisees were teaching and practising.

The heart of the matter

David gives us further insight into what it means to be 'pure in heart'. The person who has a pure heart 'does not lift up his soul to an idol or swear by what is false' (Psalm 24:4b). In other words, we are to be true to God and true to man. Our relationships with both are to be absolutely and completely sincere, with no hint of deceit or deviousness. Everything which stems from our hearts, including our thoughts and motives, should be pure and unsullied by hypocrisy or guile.

This is what God expects of us, but we all know that there are times when we fall short of such purity. But the very fact that this bothers us to the point where we come to God to ask for cleansing shows that we have hearts which are seeking to please Him. As A. W. Pink puts it: 'One of the most conclusive evidences that we do possess a pure heart is to be conscious of and burdened with the impurity which still indwells us.' Only Jesus Himself never needed to have His heart purified.

Jesus knows the importance of the heart, and has a great deal to say about it. For example: it is the source of all that we think, say and do (Matthew 5:28, 12:34, 15:18, 19); it can become hardened to God's tender touch (Matthew 13:15a); it is where doubt can take root, banishing faith (Mark 11:22, 23). No wonder He commands us to '"Love the Lord your God with all your heart"' (Matthew 22:37, Mark 12:30, Luke 10:27).

We live in a world where deceit, deviousness, hypocrisy and guile all seem to be part and parcel of life and relationships. Being pure in heart is not high on many people's agendas. As Thomas Watson observed: 'Most men pray more for full purses than for pure hearts.' And if we are not very careful, we can find ourselves being tempted to live in a similar way. We need to pray that God will give us the strength and resolve to guard the purity, integrity and sincerity of our hearts. As R. A. Torrey said: 'God does not demand a beautiful vessel, but He does demand a clean one.'

Access

The promise to the pure in heart is that they will 'see God'. According to David, the importance of having a 'pure heart' was so that a person might 'ascend the hill of the Lord' and 'stand in his holy place' (Psalm 24:3, 4). It is the pure in heart who have access into God's presence, and see Him there by the eye of faith. The writer of the letter to the Hebrews echoes David's words as he takes up this theme: 'Therefore, brothers, since we have confidence to enter the Most Holy Place by the blood of Jesus . . . let us draw near to God with a sincere heart' (Hebrews 10:19, 22a).

The exciting truth is that those who have pure and sincere hearts can access the most holy place of God's presence to see and talk to Him just as surely as they see and talk to their closest friends. That is the sense in which the 'pure in heart' can 'see God', until that great day when they see Him face to face.

* Peacemaking
In personal relationships

The seventh characteristic is that of being a peacemaker (9). There are two aspects to this. Firstly, God expects us to make sure that we, as members of His Kingdom, are living in peace with everyone. On another occasion, Jesus commands: '"be at peace with each other"' (Mark 9:50). The apostle Paul writes: 'If it is possible, as far as it depends on you, live at peace with everyone' (Romans 12:18). When he wrote to Titus, who was working as the leader of the church on the island of Crete, he said: 'Remind the people . . . to be peaceable' (Titus 3:1, 2), which was particularly appropriate, given the reputation of the Cretans for being anything but peaceable. He refers to the importance of living together in peace on other occasions too

(1 Corinthians 7:15b; 2 Corinthians 13:11; 1 Thessalonians 5:13b), and begins every one of his epistles with a greeting of peace.

The writer of the epistle to the Hebrews exhorts his readers: 'Make every effort to live in peace with all men' (Hebrews 12:14). In his letter, James reflects Proverbs 3:17, which reveals that the way of wisdom is the way of peace, when he says: 'But the wisdom that comes from heaven is . . . peace-loving . . . Peacemakers who sow in peace raise a harvest of righteousness' (James 3:17, 18). In his epistle, Peter quotes from Psalm 34:14 when he writes; 'seek peace and pursue it' (1 Peter 3:11).

• A chalk line and a dry crust

The implication of all these statements is that if we are not living in peace with everyone, then we are to take the initiative, do something about it, and be reconciled to the person or people concerned. Unlike the two unmarried sisters who had argued bitterly and had subsequently stopped talking to each other. Notwithstanding, they continued to live in the same house and to share the same rooms and the same bedroom. A chalk line divided the house into two halves for living and sleeping purposes, so that each sister could come and go and get her own meals without trespassing on the domain of the other. For years they coexisted in complete silence. Neither of them was willing to take the first step towards being reconciled.

What a sad picture this conjures up. Yet in how many families is it replicated? Maybe each sister considered that such a move would be evidence of weakness. This is certainly the viewpoint of many in our world, where capitulation rather than reconciliation is so often sought. But as Pope Paul VI once said: 'Reconciliation is not weakness or cowardice. It demands courage, nobility, generosity, sometimes heroism, an overcoming of oneself rather than of one's adversary.' We have to want to be reconciled, and God expects to see us exhibiting such a desire.

However, as the quotations from Psalm 34:14 and Hebrews 12:14 indicate, restoring peace in our relationships not only requires willing hearts, but also time, energy and determination: and then we have to work at *keeping* the peace. God expects us to be both peace-makers and peace-keepers. King Solomon is seemingly drawing on personal experience of the desirability of maintaining peaceful relationships within the family as he observes with an almost audible sigh: 'Better a dry crust with peace and quiet than a house full of feasting, with strife' (Proverbs 17:1).

• 'For the sake of food'

But our natural family is not the only place where there is conflict: sadly, it also happens in the family of God. The apostle Paul had to write to the church in Rome about a particular issue that was dividing the people into two distinct camps: food. They were at loggerheads over which foods it was permissible to eat, and which it wasn't. One group were quite happy to eat anything and everything, whereas the other group wouldn't eat certain foods for all sorts of reasons, and maintained that the rest of the church shouldn't either. The atmosphere that this was creating in the church can be easily imagined. Paul pleads with them: 'make every effort to do what leads to peace. . . . Do not destroy the work of God for the sake of food' (Romans 14:19, 20a).

I wonder how often in our churches we are guilty of 'destroying the work of God for the sake of food'? Of course serious issues, concerning for example false doctrine and immorality, must be confronted: but how often does the family of God polarise into opposite camps over disagreements that don't really matter? How many churches have split apart over relatively minor issues, to the detriment of the Gospel witness in the community? Paul's entreaty to the people of God is as relevant today as it was then.

Jesus' command to be at peace with one another extends not only to the family and to the church, but also to the workplace, and anywhere else where or when we relate to people, such as in our leisure activities. All these areas present their own difficulties, and we need to ask God constantly to strengthen us and give us the grace that is required to be faithful and obedient to His commands in all our personal relationships.

In relationships between others

The second aspect to this is that God expects us to take every opportunity to bring about reconciliation between others. This is well illustrated by the story of a church deacon, who knew that two members of the church were at loggerheads over a particular matter. We'll call them Smith and Jones.

Having prayed that God would help him to be a peacemaker, the deacon called on Smith, and asked,

'What do you think of Jones?'

'He's the meanest man in the neighbourhood!' replied Smith.

'But,' said the deacon, 'you have to admit that he's very kind to his family.'

'Oh, sure, he's kind to his family all right; no one can deny that,' said Smith.

The next day the deacon went to Jones and inquired, 'Do you know what Smith said about you?'

'No, but I can imagine how that rascal would lie about me!' replied Jones.

'This may surprise you, but he said you're very kind to your family,' said the deacon.

'What! Did Smith say that?' asked Jones, rather taken aback.

'Yes, he did,' confirmed the deacon.

'Well, if you hadn't told me, I wouldn't believe it,' said Jones.

'What do you think of Smith?' asked the deacon.

'Truthfully, I believe he's a bit of a rascal,' replied Jones.

'But you have to admit that he's very honest in business,' the deacon continued.

'Yes, there's no getting around that; in business he's a man you can trust,' admitted Jones.

The next day the deacon called on Smith again. 'You know what Jones said about you? He claims you're a fellow who really can be trusted in business, and that you're scrupulously honest.'

'You mean it?' asked Smith, surprised.

'Yes, I do', said the deacon.

'Well, of all things,' replied Smith with a smile.

The next Sunday, the former 'enemies' were seen shaking hands and talking happily together, while the peacemaker rejoiced over the reconciliation that had been brought about in answer to his prayer.

The expectation that we are to be peacemakers is an awesome challenge, be it in our families, our church, our place of work, or in the wider community. The story is told of a young daughter who was working so diligently at her homework that her father became curious and asked her what she was doing.

'I'm writing a report on the condition of the world and how to bring peace,' she replied.

'Isn't that a big order for a young girl?' her father asked.

'Oh, no,' she answered, 'and don't worry. There are three of us in the class working on it!'

The cost of peace

The promise to peacemakers is that 'they will be called sons of God'. This is because we are following the example of Jesus, who reconciled us to Himself by His death on the cross. No longer are we God's enemies, but peace has broken out between us because He took the initiative and we responded. The apostle Paul expresses it in this way: 'For God was pleased . . . through him to reconcile to himself all things . . . by making peace through his blood, shed on the cross. Once you were alienated from God and were enemies in your minds because of your evil behaviour. But now he has reconciled you by Christ's physical body through death to present you holy in his sight, without blemish' (Colossians 1:19-22).

Interestingly, the same verb which is used here to describe what God has done, and is translated 'making peace', is the very same verb used in this beatitude to describe what we should be doing: making peace and seeking reconciliation with people.

Jesus paid the ultimate price for our reconciliation and peace with God. And as we strive to bring about peace and reconciliation, there will also be a cost to us. It will cost us our pride and self-centredness as we seek to restore our personal relationships. It will cost us time and effort to understand sympathetically the points of view of those involved in a conflict in which we are seeking to mediate, and sometimes we may even find the protagonists turning on us.

However, seeking peace and reconciliation will rarely cost us our lives. Unfortunately, though, that's exactly what happened to the Israeli prime minister Yitzhak Rabin. His last public words were of a warrior turned peacemaker. Just ninety minutes before he was assassinated, he addressed a peace rally attended by an estimated 100,000 people in Tel Aviv's Kings of Israel Square, and he joined in the singing of peace songs. These were some of his final words: 'I was a military man for twenty-seven years. I waged war as long as there was no chance for peace. I believe there is now a chance for peace, a great chance, and we must take advantage of it.'

May we also be prepared to take advantage of every opportunity to be peacemakers, no matter what the cost.

* Joyful

The eighth characteristic is that of being joyful, even when we are being persecuted for our faith (10-12). During the second half of the first century AD, when the gospel accounts were written down, persecution of Christians was very much a reality, coming as it did from both the Romans and the Jews. So these particular words of Jesus would have brought great comfort, yet at the same time great challenges into the lives of the Christian believers, as they suffered for the sake of the Gospel and their allegiance to Jesus.

The blood of the martyrs

We know from the book of The Acts of the Apostles that Stephen was the first Christian martyr (Acts 7:54-60), closely followed by James Zebedee, one of the twelve disciples (Acts 12:1, 2). According to Fox's *Book Of Martyrs*, these events took place in AD44. That same book also details the martyrdoms of others of the twelve disciples, who would have heard these words of Jesus at firsthand. Philip was crucified at Heliopolis, in present-day Turkey, in the year AD54. Matthew was killed with a battleaxe in Nabadah, Ethiopia, in AD60. Andrew was crucified at Edessa in Asia. Peter was crucified upside down, possibly in Rome. Thaddaeus was crucified at Edessa in AD72. Bartholomew was cruelly beaten and then crucified in India. Thomas was speared to death, also in India. Simon the Zealot was crucified in Britain in AD74. This means that, of the twelve disciples, only John Zebedee and James Alphaeus escaped violent deaths. Even Matthias, who was chosen to replace Judas Iscariot (Acts 1:23-26), was stoned in Jerusalem prior to being beheaded.

We are also told that other well-known figures of the New Testament were martyred for their faith. James, the brother of Jesus, writer of the epistle that bears his name, and head of the church in Jerusalem (Acts 15:13-21), was stoned and clubbed to death by Jews in his old age. Mark, the writer of the second gospel, was killed in Alexandria, Egypt. The apostle Paul was beheaded with a sword, probably in Rome. Luke, the writer of the third gospel and the book of Acts, was supposedly hanged on an olive tree in Greece.

How many of these details are accurate and how much is legend or tradition we cannot be sure, but it clearly illustrates that persecution was a fact of life in the Early Church. And down through the centuries, wherever the Gospel has been preached, persecution has been the inevitable result, as the *Book Of Martyrs* goes on to illustrate.

And still today, Christians in many parts of the world are being persecuted daily for their faith by those who govern the countries in which they live. Some are being put to death. According to 'Open Doors World Watch', the top 20 countries for the persecution of Christians, in descending order, are: Saudi Arabia, Afghanistan, Sudan, China, Yemen, Morocco, Iran, Libya, Tunisia, Egypt, Uzbekistan, Vietnam, Chechnya, Pakistan, Laos, Maldives, Qatar, Turkmenistan, North Korea and Somalia. I find this statement made by a Turkmen believer very moving: 'I know that I take a great risk sharing the Gospel. I have been arrested and kept in prison overnight. Next time I will be fined a year and a half's wages. But no punishment will ever stop me.'

Three-pronged assault

Although Jesus knew the fate that awaited many of those to whom He was speaking that day, He was not just thinking of those who would be martyred. He was addressing His words to all those who would suffer persecution in any shape or form down the years until His return. Most of us will not be put to death for our faith in Christ, but we can all expect to face persecution in some form or another. This is because we are standing for what is right in God's sight in a world whose culture, outlook, values, morals and lifestyle are completely at odds with God's 'righteousness' (10). Nor can this world understand people who are prepared to be persecuted, because being popular and having easy lives are things that matter to the world in general.

The rulers of some countries are still seeking to eliminate all those who uphold this righteousness, just as the apostle Paul did before his dramatic conversion (Acts 26:9-18). However, the majority of us are more likely to face opposition in one or more of the forms identified by Jesus in verse 11. Here he outlines a three-pronged assault that we can expect: aggravation, intimidation, and defamation.

Aggravation comes in the form of insults, sneering and mocking, calculated to wind us up to the point where we either say or do something that denies what we profess to believe. Intimidation is persecution in action, and it can come in any combination of four different forms: physical, intellectual, emotional and social. These are calculated to induce feelings of fear, inferiority, isolation, and rejection, with the intention of making us crumble and renounce what we believe. Defamation is the act of spreading lies and malicious gossip in a calculated attempt to malign our characters and to undermine our integrity, thus compromising our witness.

'Because of me'

But we are not alone in times of such opposition. Jesus is walking with us and strengthening us, since He knows and understands that we are suffering, in His own words, 'because of me' (11). Thomas Watson said: 'Persecution is the legacy bequeathed by Christ to His people.' This is the cost of following Jesus and identifying ourselves with Him. As Jesus Himself said to His disciples on another occasion: '"If the world hates you, keep in mind that it hated me first. If you belonged to the world, it would love you as its own. As it is, you do not belong to the world, but I have chosen you out of the world. That is why the world hates you. . . . If they persecuted me, they will persecute you also. . . . They will treat you in this way because of my name"' (John 15:18-21).

Fitsum Gezahegne Lakew, a pastor in Ethiopia, explains the reality of the situation which faces new converts in that country today: 'When a young person comes to know Jesus, he has to choose: Jesus or his family; Jesus or his job; Jesus or his friends.' Very few of us are ever faced with such stark choices, and we need to pray continually for our brothers and sisters in countries where persecution is an integral part of their daily lives.

Response

There are various ways that we may respond to persecution. Feeling sorry for ourselves, running away from it, putting up with it and pretending it isn't happening are some of them. While, if we are feeling very brave, the thought of retaliation may even cross our minds. Yet none of these is the reaction that God expects of us. Incredibly, we are to 'Rejoice and be glad' (12a). In Luke's account, Jesus goes on to say that we should 'leap for joy' (Luke 6:23). This is definitely not my immediate response in such a situation, I must admit.

But the disciples certainly took this command of Jesus to heart. On one occasion, the Sanhedrin, who were the ruling Jewish Council in Jerusalem, 'called the apostles in and had them flogged. Then they ordered them not to speak in the name of Jesus, and let them go. The apostles left the Sanhedrin, rejoicing because they had been counted worthy of suffering disgrace for the Name. Day after day, in the temple and from house to house, they never stopped teaching and proclaiming the good news that Jesus is the Christ' (Acts 5:40, 41).

There are two points to notice here. The first is that they rejoiced because they realised what an honour and privilege it was to suffer on behalf of the Name through which we have salvation (Romans 10:13). The challenge to us is this: whenever we suffer persecution, do we show this mark of true discipleship? Dietrich Bonhoeffer, a German pastor imprisoned by the Nazis in Flossenburg concentration camp, wrote these words: 'Suffering, then, is the badge of true discipleship . . . .

Discipleship means allegiance to the suffering Christ, and it is therefore not at all surprising that Christians should be called upon to suffer. In fact, it is a joy and a token of His grace.' He was executed in April 1945, only a few days before the camp was liberated. The fact that he was shot on the direct order of Heinrich Himmler shows the extent of his impact on the Nazis, which brings us to the next point.

Secondly, they rejoiced because they realised the implications of the persecution that they were suffering. What it actually meant was that they had to be having an enormous impact on society around them, and being very effective in their witness, if the authorities were bothering to take such drastic measures against them. So they carried on with what they were doing, and the church continued to increase in numbers. The challenge to us is clear: are our churches and our own individual lives impacting society around us to the extent that we are experiencing both growth and opposition? If not, perhaps it is worth considering whether we have lost our cutting edge.

When we do experience persecution, we are in the same situation as that faced by the prophets of old (12b). They lived lives that were pleasing to God, spoke the truth of God's word to the people, and finished up being persecuted, because the people couldn't handle God's truth and wanted to get rid of it. Jeremiah is a good example of such a prophet. But the best example is Jesus Himself, who from Gethsemane to Golgotha suffered the three-pronged assault, and more besides, in man's effort to get rid of God's Truth.

Two for one

In this final beatitude, Jesus gives *two* promises to those who are persecuted. The first is that 'theirs is the kingdom of heaven' (10b). Interestingly, this is exactly the same promise made in the first beatitude to the poor in spirit. Jesus' teaching in this section has thus come full circle, as He deliberately links these two beatitudes together. In this way, Jesus makes it clear that to become members of the Kingdom of Heaven requires us not only to throw ourselves on God's mercy, which was costly for Him, but also to live lives of righteousness in society, which is costly for us.

The other promise is 'great is your reward in heaven' (12). The parable of the Talents teaches us that God rewards faithfulness, as the Master welcomes the first two servants with the words: 'Well done, good and faithful servant' (Matthew 25:21, 23). For me, those words are the most wonderful reward anyone could hope to receive.

Questions for group study

Matthew 5:3-12

Verse 3
Discuss
1. What does it mean to be 'poor in spirit'?
2. How does the parable of the Pharisee and the Tax Collector help our understanding of this beatitude?
3. How does this characteristic contrast with what we find in society?

Apply
4. Why is it important that we are 'poor in spirit'?

Verse 4
Discuss
5. What is meant by having a contrite heart?
6. What references are there to this in the Bible?

Apply
7. What can we learn from them?

Discuss
8. Why doesn't there seem to be a sense of sin, guilt and shame in society any more?
9. What are some of the consequences of this?

Apply
10. How should we react when we see such things? (See Psalm 119:136).
11. What comfort can we gain from Revelation 21:4, 5?

Verse 5
Discuss
12 What does the word 'meek' mean?
13 How can such people possibly 'inherit the earth'?
14 What examples are there of the meekness of Jesus?

Apply
15 How can we show gentleness, humility and consideration in our daily lives?
16 What can we learn from the fact that the word 'meek' is also used to describe a person who is disciplined and teachable rather than wild and self-willed?

Discuss
17 Why did Jesus get so angry about what was happening in the Court of the Gentiles?

Apply
18 What can we learn about meekness from this incident?
19 How can we put this particular aspect of meekness into practice in society?

Verse 6
Discuss
20 For what is the world around us 'hungry and thirsty'?
21 What different aspects of righteousness are there?

Apply
22 How can we put each one of them into practice in our lives?

Discuss

23 What parallel is there between physical and spiritual hunger?

Apply

24 How can we know whether or not we have an appetite for righteousness?

Verse 7

Discuss

25 What does being merciful actually mean?
26 Why does the world perceive showing mercy to be a sign of weakness?

Apply

27 How should our view of mercy differ from that of the world around us?

Discuss

28 What is the promise to those who show mercy?
29 What is the consequence for those who do not? (See James 2:13).
30 Why is the servant in the parable condemned? (See Matthew 18:23-35).

Apply

31 What can we learn from the fate of the servant?
32 How can we 'love mercy' (Micah 6:8) in our lives?

Verse 8

Background

33 To what does the phrase 'pure in heart' always refer in Scripture? (See Psalm 51:10; 24:4a).

Discuss

34 How did this beatitude cut right across what the Pharisees were teaching and practising? (See Matthew 23:25-28).

Apply

35 How does Psalm 24:4b help us to apply the concept of inward purity to our lives?

Discuss

36 In what sense can the pure in heart 'see God'?

Apply

37 What does this mean for us?

Verse 9

Background

38 Look up some of these references to living in peace with others: Mark 9:50; Romans 12:18; Titus 3:1, 2; 1 Corinthians 7:15b; 2 Corinthians 13:11; 1 Thessalonians 5:13b; Hebrews 12:14; James 3:17, 18; 1 Peter 3:11.

Discuss

39 Why is it hard to live in peace with everyone?
40 Why is it so difficult to make peace and be reconciled to others?

Apply

41 What factors are key to restoring peace in our relationships?

42 Is the atmosphere in our church one of peace and reconciliation?

43 Are there any relatively minor issues in our church which are threatening to destroy our unity as God's people?

Discuss

44 What problems arise when we try to bring about reconciliation between others?

45 Why are peacemakers promised that they 'will be called sons of God'?

Apply

46 Jesus paid the ultimate price for our reconciliation and peace with God. What may it cost us to bring about peace and reconciliation between others?

Verses 10-12

Background

47 How would these words of Jesus have brought both great comfort and great challenge into the lives of Christian believers during the second half of the first century AD?

Apply

48 What can we do to help those Christians who are suffering persecution for their faith?

Discuss

49 Why can we all expect to face persecution?

50 What three forms of persecution did Jesus identify in verse 11?

51 In what ways do these often appear?

Apply

52 How best can we meet the challenges which such persecution presents?

53 What comfort can we take from these verses when faced with such times of persecution?

Discuss

54 Why does Jesus expect us to respond to persecution with rejoicing?

55 For what two reasons did the apostles rejoice when they were persecuted? (See Acts 5:40, 41.)

Apply

56 Can we rejoice for the same reasons?

57 What implication could be drawn if our church is not experiencing any opposition?

Discuss

58 What is significant about the first of the two promises given to those who are persecuted?

Apply

59 What implications does that have for us?

For personal prayer and reflection

Do I daily acknowledge my need of God, and thank Him for my salvation?
Do I weep over my own sins and the evil in the world?
Do I need to become more disciplined and teachable?
How could I get more involved in social issues?
Do I need to develop a greater appetite for righteousness?
Do I love and practise mercy?
Is everything that stems from my heart unsullied by hypocrisy, guile or deceitfulness?
Is there someone to whom I need to be reconciled?
Am I prepared to bear the cost of helping others to become reconciled?
In what ways can the times of persecution I may experience be a cause for rejoicing?

CHAPTER 2

Sprinkled and Shining

Matthew 5:13-16; 6:22, 23

Introduction
Once again, Jesus teaches His followers by using common everyday items as illustrations, just as He did in the parables. Everybody used salt and lit lamps. Jesus now uses these two symbols of salt and light to show that God expects us to be actively involved in society, influencing it for the good.

Salt (13)

That little blue bag
One of my childhood memories is of a packet of plain potato crisps with a very small blue bag inside. On first coming across this, I thought some foreign body had invaded my snack, until I found out that this blue bag actually contained salt which was to be sprinkled over the crisps to bring out their flavour, thus

making them taste better. As I remember, this was quite a tricky operation, and could often result in some of the crisps being well salted, and others missing out altogether. When I tasted the liberally sprinkled ones, I was certainly aware of the influence of the salt. The trick was to shake the bag so that the crisps jumped up and down and all got 'influenced'. But for some reason I never seemed to manage this very well.

The days of that little blue bag of salt are long gone. Now we can choose from a vast range of flavours which have been applied at the factory. But when we taste and eat the crisps, we are still very much aware of the distinctive influence that has been brought to bear on them.

Jesus tells His followers, 'You are the salt of the earth' (13a). This means that He expects us, both individually and collectively, to have a distinctive influence on the world around us, changing society for the better. This is not an 'optional extra': this is part and parcel of being a disciple, and is a characteristic He expects to see in each one of His followers. Jesus has placed upon us both an obligation and a responsibility to the society in which we live.

Mixed in and mixing it

When salt is used in cooking, it becomes a part of the mixture, influencing it from within. In the same way, we are to be 'in the mix' of everyday life. There are two ways we can do this. Firstly, by involving ourselves fully in our individual places of work, thus becoming influences for good there, with the potential to become agents of change for the better. We need Christians in all walks of life: not just in high-profile occupations such as politics, education, and medicine. We need there to be a Christian influence in every kind of job or task that we can think of. We may not feel that we are accomplishing much, but God wants us there as His influence in that place, and will create opportunities for us. As the apostle Paul said: 'Make the most of every opportunity. Let your conversation be always . . . seasoned with salt' (Colossians 4:5, 6).

The second way is by involving ourselves collectively as a church in society and 'mixing it', as they say in the boxing world, with the problems and issues it presents. This boxing analogy gives us further insight into our involvement in society. Yes, it will be a fight to change things for the better, and we won't win every contest we enter. But enter we must, and fight we must to oppose all that is evil in society, taking a courageous stand for what is right. And we must not give up when we get knocked down, but come out fighting once again.

Sprinkled and distinctive

Let's return to that little blue bag in my packet of crisps to consider three further points.

Firstly, the bag had to be opened and the contents sprinkled for the salt to become influential. Salt works only by contact. As long as it remained in the bag, the salt was indeed present, but it was totally ineffectual. Unfortunately, this is a telling picture of many churches today. As John Stott memorably puts it: 'Christian salt has no business to remain snugly in elegant little ecclesiastical salt cellars.' We could extend this to apply to us as individuals too. May we be prepared to be open to God, and to be opened by God, so that we may be shaken out of our little blue bags, not to mention our 'ecclesiastical salt cellars', and sprinkled into the world around us, which so desperately needs to experience the influence of the salt of God's people.

Secondly, there were parts of my packet of crisps that were

well salted, while others remained virtually untouched. Maybe we are being salt in certain areas of society, but there are many others that we could and should be involving ourselves with. Perhaps we need to review exactly which areas we are influencing at the moment, and identify areas that at present stand untouched, with a view to sprinkling salt there.

Thirdly, although that little blue bag was in the packet, it was quite separate and distinct from the crisps. In the same way, both individually and collectively we as 'the salt' are quite distinct from 'the earth' (13). We are to be in the world, but not of it (John 17:15-18). Jesus is warning His followers to be on their guard about this when He says: ' "But if the salt loses its saltiness, how can it be made salty again? It is no longer good for anything, except to be thrown out and trampled by men" ' (13). My understanding is that the only way salt can lose its saltiness and become useless is if it becomes contaminated by being mixed with other impure substances. If we are to be used by God and to be influential for Him as we interact with society, we must preserve our distinctive Christian characters and attitudes, and not become indistinguishable from the world around us. And the influence that we have should be quite distinctive from any other influence that would seek to change society.

Preservation and prevention

When they were young, my two sons would always insist that a visit to relatives in Essex was incomplete without going for the umpteenth time to Colchester castle. Fortunately, it is a fascinating place to look round, and I did actually rather enjoy our excursions there. But what particularly sticks in my mind after all these years is the salt cellar. It's more of a room than a cellar, and it is huge. It was where they used to store the animal carcasses, all rubbed with salt and packed round with more salt to stop them decaying. Then when they wanted some meat, they would wash all the salt out, and find it in excellent condition for eating, thanks to the salt.

Not only is salt a condiment; it is also a preservative which prevents or arrests decay and deterioration. This reveals another aspect of Jesus' teaching about our being salt. We live in a world which is rotten with sin, and is deteriorating as a result. We see the signs of this decay all around us. Our God-given task is to be salt in this rotting carcass and to seek to arrest this decay. John Stott says that 'our place is to be rubbed into the secular community, as salt is rubbed into meat, to stop it going bad.' There will be occasions when we can expect strong reactions, particularly when sensitive areas are touched by the salt.

When the salt is rubbed in, it has a beneficial and lasting effect on the meat. Getting rubbed into our communities and places of work often takes a great deal of time and effort, but, empowered by the Holy Spirit, the effects can be amazing and glorifying to God. And who knows what evils we are preventing by being rubbed in right where we are? One thing is for sure: if it were not for the salt of many generations of Christians before us being present in society, the world would be in a far worse state than it is today.

Light (14-16)

Within and without

Jesus goes on to tell His followers, 'You are the light of the world' (14a). This means that both individually and collectively we have an obligation and a responsibility to be lights shining for God and beaming the truth of the Gospel into the darkness of the world. This is a characteristic that Jesus expects to see in all of His followers.

It is interesting to note that whereas salt works from within, light shines from without. In other words, Jesus expects us to work from the inside out, and at the same time to shine from the outside in. Talking about salt and light, R. T. France points out that: 'each is essential, but has its necessary effect on its environment only if it is both distinctive from it and yet fully involved in it.' To have an impact on the world, we must be involved in the world. As Dr Howard Hendricks says: 'It's pretty hard to be effective if you're not at a place where the salt makes contact and where the light can be seen.'

Kettles and corners

That this world is in darkness is beyond doubt. Our newspapers and television screens declare this fact daily. Of course, the world itself doesn't think it's in darkness. Rather, it considers itself to be enlightened. The apostle Paul tells us that this is because 'The god of this age has blinded the minds of unbelievers, so that they cannot see the light of the gospel of the glory of Christ' (2 Corinthians 4:4). Satan comes as an angel of light (11:14) and deceives people into thinking that his lies are the truth. He doesn't care which of his many lies they accept, provided they swallow one of them.

Jesus unequivocally declared Himself to be the Light of the world (John 9:5). And we are to reflect this light to the world. A Bible teacher named Keith Brooks had just finished speaking to a large class of businessmen on the Christian's responsibility to be a 'light' in the world. He emphasised that believers are to reflect the Light of the world, the Lord Jesus. Afterwards, one of the men told him about an experience he had at home which had impressed this same truth upon him. He said that one day when he went into his cellar he made an interesting discovery. Some potatoes had sprouted in the darkest corner of the room. At first he couldn't work out how they had got enough light to grow. Then he noticed that the cook had hung a copper kettle from the ceiling near the window in the cellar. She kept it so brightly polished that it had acted like a mirror, reflecting the rays of the sun on to the potatoes. The businessman told Mr Brooks that when he saw the kettle, he realised that, although he might not be a preacher, he could at least be a copper kettle catching the rays of the Son and reflecting His light to someone in a dark corner.

Which reminds me of that old song I learnt as a child which goes:

> 'Jesus bids us shine with a pure clear light,
> Like a little candle burning in the night.
> In this world is darkness, so we must shine –
> You in your small corner, and I in mine.'

Certainly, everyone has his own corner into which to 'shine': an area of influence that only he as an individual has the opportunity to illuminate for God. But it is important not to lose sight of the fact that we are part of a team which is reflecting God's light into society.

Saints and windows

There is another way of understanding what it means to shine as a light in the world. A young boy was visiting various cathedrals around Europe with his parents. He saw the huge stained-glass windows depicting the disciples and others regarded as saints. He was well impressed as he stood in those vast halls looking through the beautiful windows. When he got back home, he told his Sunday School teacher all about the windows with the portraits of the disciples and the saints. She asked him what he thought a saint was. He recalled standing in the cathedral looking at those huge windows, and replied: 'A saint is a man the light shines through.'

The challenge to each one of us is this: Can people see the light of God shining through my life?

Take the stand

Jesus goes on to make it clear that we should be shining as lights out in the open where everyone can see us, not hiding ourselves away in the security of our homes and churches. He uses the example of a city on a hill, which can be seen for miles around, to emphasise the point (14b). Then He follows that by saying, ' "Neither do people light a lamp and put it under a bowl" ' (15a). Such an action would be both pointless and ridiculous. ' "Instead they put it on its stand, and it gives light to everyone in the house" ' (15b). The whole purpose of lighting a lamp is so that it can shed its light abroad for the benefit of everyone.

' "In the same way," ' continues Jesus, ' "let your light shine before men" ' (16a). Unless we are prepared to take the stand so that the light of God might be shed abroad, we become pointless and ridiculous. Pointless, because the whole purpose of God's shining His light into our lives, and drawing us to Him, is that we may shine His light out to others, so they also may be drawn to Him. Ridiculous, because this light is what the world is desperately seeking, and we are hiding it away in our homes and church buildings. Dietrich Bonhoeffer commented bluntly:

'A community of Jesus which seeks to hide itself has ceased to follow Him.'

There's a light under my bucket . . .

In his translation, J. B. Phillips uses the word 'bucket' in place of 'bowl' (15). For me, this conveys more vividly the idea of hiding our light, and got me thinking about various 'buckets' we can be guilty of using.

For example: the bucket of silence, when we should have spoken out during that conversation or discussion; the bucket of conformity, when we adapted our lifestyle to fit in with the others around us; the bucket of inaction, when we couldn't be bothered to help someone who was in trouble; the bucket of denial, when we did or said something that went against what we profess to believe. And I'm sure there are many other buckets besides.

Yes in-deed

When I was a boy, I joined the local Cub group, where I learnt that I must 'keep the law of the wolf cub pack, and do a good turn to somebody every day'. All very commendable and well intentioned, but it often degenerated into doing something 'good' for the sake of it, and primarily for my benefit rather than that of the recipient of the good turn. There was a Thank-goodness-that's-my-good-deed-done-for-today-so-I-can-still-call-myself-a-cub attitude about it all. We weren't doing those good deeds because we really wanted to, but rather because we had to.

As Christians, we need to beware of this mentality. We are not to do these 'good deeds' because we feel obliged to do them, or so that we can feel good about ourselves; but rather so that others may see them, benefit from them, and thereby encounter the light of God's compassion shining in us and through us. The result of our actions should impact people to the extent that they praise God and come to know Him for themselves (16b).

Jesus had more to say about the importance of deeds in the parable of the Sheep and the Goats (Matthew 25:31-46). There, as here, the challenge is to consider the extent to which we as churches are involved in social action locally. Can the community around us actually see our good deeds?

And light is attractive. You have only to open a window and switch on a light when it's dark to prove that; suddenly, the room is invaded by great big moths and other insects, all of which are attracted to the light. And how much more attractive a well-lit room is to a dark one. Bearing this in mind, we need to ask whether our church is attractive to the community, drawing people to it by its good deeds, and thereby bringing them to Christ.

Lighthouses and torches

Letting our light shine also involves *telling* people about the good news of God's love as well as *showing* them His love through our good deeds. In this sense of bringing the Gospel message, we could be described as being like lighthouses taking our stand on the rock Christ Jesus. The light which shines out from us shows people the way to God, and also points out the dangers of the many rocks on which they can run aground.

The result of hearing the Gospel is that people praise God for it and respond to it. They are going to do that only if it is communicated to them in the right way, so we need to take great care over how we present its message. Certainly we should not compromise it in any way, but at the same time we must be wise and sensitive in how we put it across, lest we cause people to turn away from the Light rather than bring them to the Light.

Coupled with this is the importance of allowing God's light to shine through us by the way we live our lives day by day. The constant cry of the world is about hypocrisy in the lives of those who claim to be Christians. We are under the world's microscope all the time. I remember an incident one day at the cricket club, in which we as a family are fully involved. Something had happened to make me really angry, and I was suddenly aware of one of the players standing a short distance away looking at me. On my asking him what he wanted, he replied, 'Nothing. I was just waiting to see if you'd swear!' I relate this not to give any credit to myself, but to illustrate how closely and minutely we can expect to be observed. It is so important that in front of everyone we live our lives in accordance with God's Word to give credence to the Gospel that we profess to believe.

If my experience is anything to go by, this is very difficult to maintain. We need God's power flowing through us to enable us to shine effectively. To think of our light as the beam of a torch using rechargeable batteries helps to illustrate the point. In order to maintain a powerful beam of light, the batteries must be recharged regularly, otherwise the light will gradually fade, grow dim, become almost imperceptible and then be extinguished. The same process will happen to our light if our lives are not regularly recharged by the power of the Holy Spirit. No wonder the apostle Paul encourages us to keep on being filled with the Spirit (Ephesians 5:18b).

There's a war on

One of my favourite characters in the comedy series 'Dad's Army' is Hodges, the ARP Warden. He struts round the town of Warmington-on-Sea each night, yelling, 'Put that light out! It can be seen for miles around!', and usually finishing up with, 'Don't you know there's a war on!'

We are involved in a different kind of war: a spiritual one. And this war is definitely on, and it is on all the time. We have an enemy who is determined for two reasons to put out that light which shines from each one of us. Firstly, because it can be seen for miles around by all the people we come into contact with; and secondly, because evil doesn't like the light of God shining into the blanket of darkness that it has created, showing it up for what it is.

We all feel that at times our light is pretty feeble, but even the smallest light has an effect. I remember as a young child being afraid of the dark as I lay in bed. So to help me relax and go to sleep, a small candle was lit and placed on the dressing-table where I could see it. Although its flame was feeble, it brought light into the dark room, and had the required effect.

Having failed to extinguish the Light of the world, Satan seeks to put out all those who reflect that light and allow it to shine through them. That he bothers to do this indicates just how threatened he feels by us, and should be of great encouragement to us to keep on shining in this world of darkness.

More light (6:22, 23)

At this point in his account, Luke records some more sayings of Jesus on the subject of light (Luke 11:34-36). Although these do not appear in Matthew until chapter 6:22, 23, they seem to me to fit in better here, so we will consider them now.

Eyes wide open

Jesus begins by saying, ' "The eye is the lamp of the body" ' (6:22a). Clearly, Jesus does not mean us to take this literally. He is making the point that we rely on our ability to see in order to carry out many of our physical activities successfully. Imagine, for example, trying to do the housework, go shopping, cook a meal, drive a car, take exercise or play sport without being able to see what you're doing. Having said that, I am full of admiration for the marvellous way in which many people who are blind seem to cope with life. But being without the advantage of good eyesight, they are in total physical darkness, in complete contrast to the sighted person. This is what Jesus is meaning when He says: ' "If your eyes are good, your whole body will be full of light. But if your eyes are bad, your whole body will be full of darkness" ' (22b, 23a).

Jesus is teaching us that what is true physically is also true spiritually. If our spiritual eyes are wide open and focused on God, we shall be able to see clearly the way He wants us to go, and what He wants us to do; everything in our lives will be in focus, and we shall be able to see things from God's perspective. Unfortunately, our spiritual vision can so easily become clouded and blurred by the things of this world and by our own sinfulness. Consequently, we lose our way, purpose and direction; things in our lives get out of focus, and our perspective becomes distorted.

When is the light not the light?

Jesus concludes by saying: ' "If then the light within you is darkness, how great is that darkness!" ' (23b.) How can the light be darkness? It seems to me that Jesus is warning us about the schemes of Satan, who, as we noted earlier in this chapter, masquerades as an angel of light. Satan does this in an attempt to deceive mankind into thinking that his way of darkness is in fact the way of light, so that we will choose to follow him instead of Christ. Many are indeed deceived by Satan's craftiness, and follow him as their light, not realising that they are in fact accepting the kingdom of darkness into their lives. And when a person's 'light' is actually darkness, then he is completely in the dark, though tragically he thinks he is in the light. Only the true light of Christ can dispel such total darkness and show it up for what it really is.

John was speaking about Jesus when he wrote these words: 'The true light that gives light to every man was coming into the world' (John 1:9). And this true light came so that none of us needs ever walk in darkness. Jesus Himself made this wonderful statement: ' "I am the light of the world. Whoever follows me will never walk in darkness, but will have the light of life" ' (John 8:12).

Questions for group study

Matthew 5:13-16; 6:22, 23

Verse 13

Discuss

1. Jesus tells us that we are 'the salt of the earth'. What obligation and responsibility does this place upon us?

Apply

2. How can we fulfil this expectation as individuals?
3. How might Paul's words in Colossians 4:5, 6 help us in this regard?
4. How can we fulfil this expectation as a church: locally, nationally and internationally?
5. Is our community experiencing the influence of the salt of God's people; or are we present, but largely ineffectual?
6. Are there areas of society that we should be seeking to influence as a church which we haven't yet touched?

Discuss

7. How is it possible for salt to lose its saltiness?

Apply

8. As we interact with society, why is it important to preserve our distinctive Christian character and attitudes, and not become indistinguishable from the world around us?
9. Why should our influence be quite distinctive from any other influence that would seek to change society?

10 What can we learn from the fact that salt is also a preservative, which prevents or arrests decay and deterioration?
11 Which areas of society do we find are particularly sensitive to having the salt applied to them?

Verse 14a
Discuss

12 Jesus also tells us that we are 'the light of the world'. What obligation and responsibility does this place upon us?
13 What fundamental difference is there between the ways that salt and light work?

Apply

14 What implications can we draw from this?

Discuss

15 Why does the world we live in consider itself to be enlightened rather than being in darkness? (See 2 Corinthians 4:4; 11:14).

Apply

16 Into what areas of society do we have the opportunity to reflect God's light?
17 In what ways should people be able to see the light of God shining through our lives?

Verses 14b-16

Discuss
18 What point is Jesus making by using the examples of the city on a hill and the lamp on a stand?

Apply
19 With what justification could it be said that, unless we are prepared to be like lamps on a stand, we become pointless and ridiculous?
20 What sort of 'buckets' to hide our light can we be guilty of using?

Discuss
21 What should be our motives for doing good deeds?

Apply
22 Can the community around us actually see our good deeds?
23 Is our church attractive to people? Does it draw them to Christ?

Discuss
24 In what sense can we be described as being like a lighthouse?
25 What should be the result of people hearing the Gospel?
26 What implications does this have for the way we present it?

Apply
27 Why is it important that we practise what we preach?
28 In this respect, why does Paul encourage us to keep on being filled with the Spirit (Ephesians 5:18b)?

Discuss
29 Why is Satan determined to stop our light from shining out into the world?

Apply
30 What encouragement can we draw from this?

Chapter 6, verses 22, 23
Discuss
31 What point is Jesus making when he says 'The eye is the lamp of the body'?

Apply
32 How does this apply to us spiritually?
33 What can happen if our spiritual vision becomes clouded and blurred?

Discuss
34 How can the light within people in fact be darkness?

For personal prayer and reflection

In what ways am I being salt in my place of work or sphere of influence?

Do I need to seize opportunities to speak to people more readily than I do?

What conversations have I had recently that I need to pray about and follow up?

Can people see a distinctiveness and an integrity about my character, attitudes and lifestyle?

Am I prepared to be 'rubbed in' right where I am, even though I may encounter strong reactions?

Can people see God's light shining through my life?

What 'buckets' do I need to remove so that my light can shine out?

Do I present an attractive picture of what it is to be a Christian?

When I present the Gospel to people, do I do so in a sensitive way?

Do I regularly ask God to fill me with the power of His Spirit so I may continue to shine effectively?

Have I carried out a spiritual eye-test recently?

CHAPTER 3

But I Tell You . . .

Matthew 5:17-48; 7:12

Jesus and the Law (17-20)

Abolitionist or Loyalist?

There is by now a growing recognition among the people that Jesus speaks and acts with an authority unlike anything they have ever witnessed before (Mark 1:22, 27; 2:10; 3:15). Such is the impact of this, that many are beginning to wonder if He is even about to overturn all that they have been taught to believe in. Jesus is quick to nip such thinking in the bud, and says categorically: ' "Do not think that I have come to abolish the Law or the Prophets; I have not come to abolish them but to fulfil them" ' (17).

The Law of Moses and the writings of the Prophets were very sacred to the Jews. The first five books of the Jewish Scriptures were covered by the term 'the Law'. They were also known as the Pentateuch. They contained all the laws given to them by God through Moses. There were ceremonial laws, civil laws and moral laws. The ceremonial laws dealt with matters of worship; the civil laws dealt with how to live together in society; the moral laws, most notably the Ten Commandments, dealt with relationships with God and with one another. The rest of the Scriptures were covered by the term 'the Prophets'. We call these Jewish Scriptures 'The Old Testament'.

Matthew records in detail what Jesus has to say about the Law and the Prophets, because he is writing his gospel with Jewish Christians in mind, and for them this is an important issue. As it is of no concern to Gentile Christians, because they have obviously not been brought up to follow the teachings of the Jewish Scriptures, the gospels of Mark and Luke pay far less attention to these matters.

Throughout His ministry Jesus never questions the divine authority of the Law. Rather than being an abolitionist, Jesus is in fact a loyalist.

Double fulfilment

But He is more than loyal to the teachings of the Law and the Prophets: He says He has come to 'fulfil' them. And He seems to do this in two particular ways.

• Teaching

Firstly, He brings out their deeper teaching and full meaning. The Sermon on the Mount gives specific examples of how He does this, and we shall be looking at these later in this chapter. And He backs up the principles He is emphasising to them by the way He lives His life. Jesus Himself is the supreme example of God's principles being put into practice.

Until now, only their surface meanings have been heeded.

The letter of the Law has been adhered to rather than the spirit of the Law being lived out. The Pharisees in particular have paid lip-service to the Law in the mistaken belief that this gives them merit and makes them righteous in God's sight, while at the same time not practising its principles in their lives. In other words, there is no depth to their obedience. Such hypocrisy has set them on a collision course with Jesus, who eventually confronts them head-on (Matthew 23:1-36). He condemns them, not just for their hypocrisy but for their failure to teach and lead the people properly (23:13), describing them as 'blind guides' (23:16).

• Prophecies
Secondly, during His life He fulfils all that these writings said about the Messiah. There is that amazing occasion in the synagogue at His home town of Nazareth, when He reads from chapter 61 of the prophet Isaiah, and then announces: ' "Today this scripture is fulfilled in your hearing" ' (Luke 4:21).

After His resurrection, Jesus appears to the disciples, 'And beginning with Moses and all the Prophets, he explained to them what was said in all the Scriptures concerning himself. . . . He said to them, "This is what I told you while I was still with you: Everything must be fulfilled that is written about me in the Law of Moses, the Prophets and the Psalms"' (Luke 24:27, 44).

Transfiguration confirmation
This is why the Transfiguration is such a significant event (Matthew 17:1-8; Mark 9:2-8; Luke 9:28-36). As Jesus is transfigured in front of their very eyes, Peter, James and John see Moses and Elijah appear 'in glorious splendour' and stand

'talking with Jesus' (Luke 9:31). Moses, the great lawgiver, obviously represented the Law. Elijah represented the prophets.

• The Law

Moses appeared there to show that Jesus in His life and death would meet all the requirements of the Law. This meant that after His death significant changes would result. The New Covenant or Testament, brought into being by the death of Jesus on the cross, would replace the Old Covenant, brought into being through Moses at Mount Sinai. Salvation would now come through our putting our faith, trust and belief in Jesus. Since Jesus is our sacrifice, no longer do we need to offer sacrifices for forgiveness, in accordance with the requirements of the ceremonial laws.

This is how the apostle Paul explains it: 'Christ is the end of the law so that there may be righteousness for everyone who believes. . . . But now a righteousness from God, apart from law, has been made known, to which the Law and the Prophets testify. This righteousness from God comes through faith in Jesus Christ to all who believe' (Romans 10:4; 3:21-22).

• The Prophets

Elijah, considered by the Jews to be the greatest of the prophets apart from Moses, appeared there to show that Jesus would fulfil all the prophecies they had made concerning the Messiah. Indeed, Matthew is at pains to point out examples of such prophecies to his Jewish readers (Matthew 2:15, 17, 23; 13:14, 35; 26:54, 56; 27:9). It is particularly in the prophecies of Isaiah that we see the role of the Messiah as God's Suffering Servant, who will die innocently for the sin of the world (Isaiah 42:1-4; 49:1-7; 52:13-53:12).

The name Jesus means 'God is salvation' (Matthew 1:21). The Hebrew form of Jesus is Joshua. Interestingly, the work of Moses was finished by Joshua; the work of Elijah was completed by Elisha, another form of the name Joshua; and Jesus, or Joshua, would bring to fulfilment the work of both Moses and Elijah.

Not a patch on it

On another occasion, Jesus used two different but related illustrations to explain what was happening (Matthew 9:16, 17; Mark 2:21, 22; Luke 5:36-39). When a garment has served its purpose, it is best to replace it with a new one, rather than try to patch it up. Patches never quite match; nor do they blend in. Better to have a new garment, whose colours and fabrics do blend, rather than a patchwork quilt of a garment, whose materials clash with one another. As Professor Stevens wrote: 'His gospel is not a patch to be sewed on to the old garment of Judaism, but a wholly new garment.'

Similarly, it is foolish to pour new wine into old wineskins. This is because the old skins have been stretched to their limit already, and when the new wine within them ferments and expands, they will burst. The 'new wine' of Christianity could not be contained within the 'old skins' of the Jewish religion. New skins were required.

Principles into practice

Unchanged

However, Jesus makes it very clear that the Law is not coming to an end, but that He has come to fulfil it. Although the requirements of the ceremonial laws would no longer be relevant, the principles behind them of loving and worshipping a God who is holy would still remain. Similarly, although the civil laws applied to a bygone age and a completely different culture, the principles behind them must still be followed in society. The moral laws remain unchanged, and we are still required by God to live according to the principles they lay down. To return to the illustration of the wineskins, the principles of the 'old wine' are to be retained (Luke 5:39).

Jesus says that these principles given to us by God Himself will remain in force 'until heaven and earth disappear' (18). Indeed, God places the highest value on each member of His kingdom who obeys, 'practises and teaches these commands': and that includes all of His laws, even 'the least' (19). As C. H. Spurgeon wrote: 'The peerage of Christ's kingdom is ordered according to obedience.'

Righteousness of heart

Jesus then goes on to say something quite extraordinary: 'For I tell you that unless your righteousness surpasses that of the Pharisees and the teachers of the law, you will certainly not enter the kingdom of heaven' (20). Undoubtedly, Jesus is being ironic about the so-called righteousness of the Pharisees and teachers of the law, because it did not gain them the favour with God that they hoped it would. However, albeit with the wrong motives, they tried to be righteous by keeping all the laws of Moses. These amounted to 248 positive and 365 negative commandments.

But their righteousness was an obedience that touched only the surface of their lives. It was self-centred, not God-centred, and was done to gain the approval and acclamation of those around them. It didn't penetrate the depths of their hearts and set the pattern for their behaviour and lifestyles. And this brings us to the point that Jesus is making here. God is not interested in or impressed by surface obedience: He is looking for something different, something deeper, something which 'surpasses' that charade. He is looking for a righteousness of the heart.

As members of the Kingdom of Heaven, we need to show that daily depth of obedience in every aspect of our lives which testifies to the fact that Jesus is our Lord, and that His law is written on our hearts (Jeremiah 31:33). The challenging question to each one of us is this: Am I putting the principles of God's law into practice in my life each day? If so, then that is evidence of a righteousness of heart, a righteousness which 'surpasses that of the Pharisees and the teachers of the law' (20). It is only by the power of the Holy Spirit, who has lived within us since we accepted Christ as our Saviour, that we can do this. This daily walk of depth obedience and righteousness of heart ends only when we enter into the fullness of that Kingdom in Heaven itself.

Examples from the Law (21-48)

Introduction

Jesus goes on to give examples of this deeper righteousness. This is to show His followers what is required of them so that they might obey the law more fully and completely than the Pharisees and the teachers of the law were doing. These examples show how Jesus fulfilled the Law by revealing its deeper meaning. Thus Jesus is giving us a greater understanding of God's thinking behind the framing of these laws.

Each time, Jesus refers to what has been said, and then continues: ' "But I tell you . . ." ' (22, 28, 32, 34, 39, 44), thus setting out what God expects of us in each situation. However, it would be a mistake to conclude from this clause that Jesus is contradicting or even nullifying the Law of Moses, particularly since He has just finished supporting it and emphasising its importance. Rather, He is giving the correct interpretation of the law in question, with all its implications, in contrast to the way that the rabbis had interpreted it down the years: namely, to suit their convenience, and to make it easier to obey.

Matthew presents

Nevertheless, to expand and extend the God-given law as Jesus now does is something that no ordinary Jew would even dare to contemplate, let alone to do. It could be argued that Matthew deliberately presents Jesus to his Jewish readers as a lawgiver greater than Moses. Indeed, W. D. Davies confirms that 'the Jesus presented by Matthew is very much like Moses.'

The law was given to Moses at Mount Sinai, so Matthew has Jesus giving the whole of this Sermon on a mountainside (5:1), whereas Luke's setting is 'a level place' (Luke 6:17). The Old Covenant was established at Mount Sinai through the giving of laws and the offering of sacrifices (Exodus 24:5-8). Here, on this mountainside, the laws of the New Covenant are being set out; the sacrifice that will consummate its establishment will happen at the place of crucifixion (Matthew 26:28; 27:33).

Some would go further, seeing a significance in the way Matthew has structured his gospel. After a Prologue, which covers the birth and the preparation for His ministry (1:1-4:17), come five 'books', each with a particular focus, as follows: Book 1 (4:18-7:29), the teaching of Jesus; Book 2 (8:1-11:1), the miracles; Book 3 (11:2-13:52), the kingdom; Book 4 (13:53-19:1), the reactions to His ministry; Book 5 (19:2-25:46), conflict with the religious leaders. These five 'books' correspond to the Pentateuch, the five books of the Law. Then comes the Epilogue, which covers the events of Passion Week through to the Ascension (26:1-28:20).

1) Murder, Anger and Reconciliation (21-26)

Jesus takes the sixth of the Ten Commandments as His first example. This states: 'You shall not murder' (Exodus 20:13). The scribes and Pharisees clearly believed, and taught the people to believe, that provided they avoided murdering anybody, they were keeping this commandment. However, Jesus is about to show that there is much more to it than that.

The heart of the problem

He identifies what is actually at the heart of the problem: namely, anger. This is not a righteous anger, which wells up in the face of some injustice or wrong that needs to be set right. Nor is it the kind of anger we all feel at times when we are very cross about something and maybe lose our temper momentarily. Not at all. This is the kind of anger which festers with resentment and seethes with bitterness against someone, and is often bound up with hatred. It is the kind of anger which, if left unchecked, can lead to murder.

But even if it doesn't go as far as that, expressions of such anger are still 'subject to judgement' (22a) in the same way that the act of murder itself is (21b). This shows us just how seriously Jesus regards this powerful emotion, which He is saying must be controlled and dealt with at source. And that source is the heart, from whence come all angry thoughts, feelings and actions.

The epistle of James tells us: 'Everyone should be . . . slow to become angry, for man's anger does not bring about the righteous life that God desires' (James 1:19, 20). The writer of the book of Proverbs recognises how powerful anger is when he says: 'He that is slow to anger is better than the mighty; and he that ruleth his spirit than he that taketh a city' (16:32, KJV). Much more recently, another writer puts it like this: 'Control yourself! Anger is only one letter short of danger.'

Insults and assassination

Apparently, the scribes and Pharisees already taught that the expression of anger through insults was unacceptable in society: 'Anyone who says to his brother, "Raca," is answerable to the Sanhedrin,' Jesus reminds them (22b). In the language of Aramaic which Jesus spoke, 'Raca' probably derives from another word meaning 'empty'. So to call someone by this term meant that you considered them to be empty-headed, intellectually challenged, or just plain thick. The Sanhedrin were the ruling Jewish council responsible for the upholding of the Jewish Law, and they could apparently take action against anyone who was guilty of perpetrating such an insult.

' "But," ' Jesus continues, ' "anyone who says 'You fool!' will be in danger of the fire of hell" ' (22c). The term for 'fool' used here is the Greek word *more*, from which we get our word 'moron'. It seems that this word referred to in Psalm 14:1-4 and 53:1-4, was used to refer to the sort of fool who refuses to believe that God exists, and consequently lives in a corrupt and evil way, which can only meet with God's judgement.

Therefore, to call someone 'you fool' is the ultimate insult, the ultimate expression of anger and hatred of a fellow human being. It represents the complete assassination of his whole being, virtually telling him that hell is where he is going. To be so angry with someone as to wish him in hell, says Jesus, is to put yourself in danger of hell. In the epistle of John we read these interesting words, which seem to reflect what Jesus is saying here: 'Anyone who hates his brother is a murderer, and you know that no murderer has eternal life in him' (1 John 3:15).

As He often does throughout His ministry, Jesus is using a dramatic example here to make His point. We may never get to the stage of wishing someone in hell, or even wishing he were dead. But it is because Jesus is so concerned that we should be on our guard against this potentially destructive emotion of anger, and deal with it as soon as it appears, that He speaks about it in such a strong way.

The way of reconciliation

Cain is perhaps the most poignant example of what can happen to a person who allows anger to dwell in his heart (Genesis 4:3-12). When God accepts his brother Abel's sacrifice but rejects his, Cain is 'very angry' (5). And, as Philip Henry wrote, 'When anger was in Cain's heart, murder was not far off.' Instead of sorting the problem out with God when given the opportunity to do so, Cain allows his heart to become consumed with resentment, bitterness and ultimately hatred towards his brother Abel; and the rest, as they say, is history.

It is easy to fall into the way of Cain, allowing anger to take root within our hearts. As we have already seen, Jesus has warned us that this will mean our being judged by God (22a);

so we need to repent and ask God's forgiveness. But that's not all. There are two other steps that must be taken. The first of these is to 'Get rid of all bitterness, rage and anger . . . along with every form of malice' (Ephesians 4:31). That is an act of our will.

The second is explained by Jesus Himself, and He does it by using two illustrations (23-26). The first concerns a brother in the temple, which for us means the church; the second involves someone who is taking us to court. In both cases, the point is the same: we must take immediate steps to put things right and be reconciled to the person concerned as soon as possible. Such an attitude is pleasing to God, and is what He expects to see in all those who are members of His Kingdom. Whether the person is a brother in Christ or an acquaintance in the world is irrelevant.

Before worship

However, the scene Jesus portrays in the temple (23, 24) does have another layer of meaning which is very significant: reconciliation needs to be made before coming to worship God, not afterwards. This is because having something against another person is an obstacle to our worshipping God with integrity. Anger, resentment, bitterness, and hatred are barriers not only between us and the person concerned, but also between us and God. That is why Jesus says, ' "First go and be reconciled to your brother; then come and offer your gift" ' (24).

Someone once said: 'A believer at war with his brother cannot be at peace with his Father.' Could that be why there are times in our lives when we don't feel close to God any more; times when our worship seems unfulfilling; times when our prayers just seem to bounce back off the ceiling? The person who really suffers during such times is not the 'brother' involved, but I.

God expects to see in us a willingness to be reconciled with others. I am not pretending that this is easy, particularly if we have been wronged and deeply hurt by the actions of another person. Forgiveness is costly but *un*forgiveness is even costlier.

There is also a particular sensitivity required of us here. We are to be aware of any distress we may have caused to others that may have made them angry towards us, and go and be reconciled to them immediately, asking their forgiveness. If the truth be told, we can readily give a whole list of things that have been done wrong to us, but rarely can we list the offences we have committed against others. Yet our desire for reconciliation should be such that not only do we approach people who have done wrong to us, but also those whom we ourselves have wronged, so that we might be reconciled to them. In doing this, we are following the example of Jesus, whom the apostle Paul tells us 'was reconciling the world to himself' (2 Corinthians 5:19).

A lesson for Leonardo

There is a story told about the famous artist Leonardo da Vinci. When he was in the process of painting 'The Last Supper', he had an intense, bitter argument with a fellow painter. Leonardo was so angry that he decided to paint the face of his enemy into the face of Judas. That way the hated painter's face would be preserved for all time in the face of the disciple who betrayed Jesus.

When Leonardo finished Judas, everyone easily recognised the face of the painter with whom Leonardo had quarrelled. He continued to work on the painting. But as much as he tried, he could not paint the face of Christ. Something was holding him back.

Eventually, Leonardo realised his hatred towards his fellow painter was the problem. So he worked through his hatred by repainting Judas' face, replacing the image of his fellow painter with another face. Only then was he able to paint Jesus' face and complete the masterpiece.

2) Adultery, Lust and Self-Control (27-30)

Jesus now moves on to talk about another equally powerful and potentially destructive emotion: sexual lust. He begins by reminding his hearers of the seventh commandment, which forbids adultery (Exodus 20:14). As was the case with the law about anger, Jesus is about to show that there is much more to this law than just avoiding adultery.

The heart of the problem

From what He goes on to say, it is clear that Jesus has in mind all forms of sexual immorality. We all know that women and unmarried men are equally as capable of being lustful as married men are. Therefore, it is inconceivable that Jesus is talking here only about married men, thus allowing women and unmarried men to be as lustful as they like. No: He is talking about the general principle of lust, which applies to everyone, and which He identifies as being at the heart of the problem of sexual immorality.

The desire for a physical relationship with a member of the opposite sex is natural and it is good. God Himself placed this drive within us so that we could experience the joy and pleasure of sex within a loving and committed relationship, husband and wife together. God made sure that a book which presents the sensuousness and delight of sex in such a context, the 'Song of Songs', was included in the canon of Scripture.

But, as with everything else God created, it can be abused. And it is, every day and in every way imaginable. Films, videos, magazines, newspapers, pop songs, and television programmes all testify to that, as they trumpet so-called 'sexual freedom' and the 'condom culture', thus fuelling the fire of lustful desire which smoulders within each one of us. When they talk about love, they mean sex; when they talk about sex they mean sport. And the concept of commitment is conspicuous by its absence.

Of course, lust has been a problem since sin entered the world, and it always will be a problem as long as sinful human beings exist. As with anger, Jesus is saying that the only way to deal with lust is to control it before it takes hold of the heart.

Catching the eye

Usually, lust is stimulated through the eye. All the media I mentioned above exploit the eye as the way into the heart, some accompanied by sound to catch the ear as well. Pop songs work the other way round, but the development of television, video and the Internet has enabled the singers to catch the eye by means of dance and dress, or rather the lack of it in the case of many girl bands.

The whole issue of how we should dress is a contentious one. Without wishing to sound sexist, I think this is a particularly difficult area for women, some of whom seem to be blissfully unaware of the profound effect that their appearance is having on the men around them. I see nothing wrong in a woman dressing fashionably and attractively, but this needs to be done wisely. It is quite possible to be prudent without being prudish. However, it is true that some women seem to enjoy being seductive and dress deliberately for effect. The newspaper columnist Richard Littlejohn expressed the sentiment that women who 'dress like prostitutes' can hardly expect to be 'treated like nuns'. In this whole matter of dress, it seems to me that the older women have a responsibility to advise and to be an example to the younger women (Titus 2:3-5).

The look

Jesus speaks of the look which stimulates the lust which takes hold of the heart, which is where the adultery takes place (28). Although there is no physical act of sex, there might just as well have been, because the intention is there. Jesus is saying that having the desire to commit the act is as wrong as the act itself; the one will ultimately lead to the other if it is not checked.

The only way to stop this adultery of the heart is to prevent lust being stimulated by the eye in the first place. The words of Job are interesting in this respect. He says: ' "I made a covenant with my eyes not to look lustfully at a girl" ' (Job 31:1). He then goes on to recognise that he deserves God's punishment ' "if my heart has been led by my eyes . . . If my heart has been enticed by a woman"' (31:7, 9). He had learnt that what the eye sees must not be allowed to become a lustful look, which will ultimately take hold of the heart.

Yet we need to keep a sense of proportion in all this, otherwise we won't dare to look a member of the opposite sex in the face ever again, just in case. That is not Jesus' intention here. Indeed, we have already seen that a healthy interest in the opposite sex is a God-given drive. And we shall continue to be struck by the attractiveness of someone of the opposite sex from time to time throughout our lives. It is not what the eye sees that is sinful, but allowing it to develop into a look of lust. What we need to be able to do is to recognise the danger signs, such as starting to become preoccupied with one particular person and beginning to have sexual fantasies about him or her, and deal with the problem then and there, before lust has a chance to take hold.

Self-control

Should we fall prey to such lust, not only do we need to repent, asking God to forgive us and to strengthen us, but we also need to take steps which will help to prevent our becoming ensnared yet again. For example, disposing of certain magazines and videos, putting some distance between ourselves and certain other persons, not watching certain programmes any more, not going to certain places ever again, and so on. As Jerry Bridges said: 'Guarding our hearts begins with guarding our eyes and ears.'

One thing we can be sure of: failure to exercise such self-control will eventually lead to disaster. Adultery destroys marriages and breaks up families, with the massive impact that has on the children involved. Sexual relationships outside of marriage always seem attractive propositions, but more often than not they have a hurtful and destructive outcome, affecting the lives of many more people than the two actually involved.

Self-control is one of the nine fruit of the Spirit (Galatians 5:22, 23). The extent to which these characteristics are evident in our lives is an indication of the degree to which we are allowing God's Spirit to work within us, making us more like Christ.

Drastic action

Jesus goes on to use two vivid illustrations to emphasise how vital self-control and self-discipline are. Clearly, He takes the subject very seriously indeed, and it is evident that He expects His followers to exercise these two key characteristics in their daily lives. In deliberately dramatic language, He commands us: ' "If your right eye causes you to sin, gouge it out and throw it away, . . . And if your right hand causes you to sin, cut it off and throw it away" ' (29a, 30a). And just to make sure His hearers have got the message, He repeats it later in His ministry, on this occasion referring to hands and feet (Matthew 18:8, 9).

Jesus is not expecting us to carry this out literally, although some have actually done so. One such person was Origen of Alexandria, a scholar who lived in the third century. In response to these verses and to what he also read in Matthew 19:12, he actually castrated himself to become a eunuch. This is not the sort of drastic action that Jesus has in mind. Rather, He is requiring us to be ruthless with anything in our lives which leads us into sin.

So, if what we see or watch causes us to sin, we must stop seeing or watching it; if what we touch or allow to come into our hands is the problem, we must stop touching or handling it; if the places we go or the paths we find ourselves walking on are leading us into sinful ways, we must stop going or walking there. As Dr Martyn Lloyd-Jones wrote: 'The great need in the Christian life is for self-discipline. This is not something that happens to you in a meeting; you have got to do it!'

Protect and save

These days, as never before, we are under tremendous pressure to watch certain films and videos, to read certain books and magazines, to go to certain places and behave in certain ways. To refuse to conform to these unwritten cultural and social requirements is bound to bring expressions of incredulity leading to scorn and even ridicule, particularly for the teenage Christian. It may be difficult to cut these things out of our lives, and the consequences of doing so may be painful, but do it we must if we are to live our lives in a way that is pleasing to God.

The fact that Jesus speaks to us in such a strong way on this subject shows how much He loves us and cares about what happens to us. He does not demand that we exercise such rigorous self-control to spoil our fun or cramp our style. Quite the opposite. Jesus wants us to enjoy life to the full and to develop to our full potential as individuals. But He also knows the dangers that await us, and wants to protect us from falling into evil ways that will do untold damage to our lives and to the lives of those around us. This applies not only to lust, but all the emotions, appetites, impulses and desires that we experience.

There is another reason as well. Jesus wants to save us from the consequences of our sinfulness, which is why He says: ' "It is better for you to lose one part of your body than for your whole body to be thrown into hell/to go into hell" ' (29b, 30b). Better to take drastic action now to prevent ourselves from falling into sin than to take no action, and consequently find ourselves under the awesome judgement of God.

3) Divorce, Hard-heartedness and Restoration (31, 32)

It is a distressing fact that nowadays four out of every ten marriages end in divorce. Having friends who have gone through this traumatic experience, and others who are in the throes of it, I am well aware just how sensitive, complex and controversial an issue this is. This means treating the subject with great care, yet at the same time having the courage and desire to understand and apply Jesus' teaching.

'Something indecent'

The two verses that we read here are basically a brief summary of Jesus' teaching on this subject, so it makes sense to examine the more detailed account of what He says, which is recorded in Matthew 19:3-9. This takes the form of a question-and-answer session between the Pharisees and Jesus. The Pharisees begin by asking Jesus: ' "Is it lawful for a man to divorce his wife for any and every reason?" ' (19:3).

There were two schools of thought within the Jewish religion on the issue of divorce. The argument centred on the interpretation of Deuteronomy 24:1, which states that a woman may be given a certificate of divorce on the grounds that the husband has found 'something indecent' about her. The dispute concerned what this phrase actually meant. The school of rabbi Shammai interpreted it as referring only to 'marital unfaithfulness': in other words, adultery or gross sexual misconduct. On the other hand, the school of rabbi Hillel taught that it meant 'for any and every reason'. This latter interpretation meant that a wife could be divorced on even the most trivial grounds, such as accidentally burning the food. Such an action was deemed to have made her 'displeasing to him' (Deuteronomy 24:1).

One plus one equals one

Jesus is far more concerned to put the focus on marriage rather than coming down on one side or the other in the great divorce debate. So, rather than answering their question directly by talking about divorce, Jesus instead reaffirms the permanence of marriage, reminding them that it was instituted by God Himself. He does this by asking them a question in reply, a technique which He often uses with the Pharisees. This question refers them back to God's original intention, which was that a man and a woman were to be united together for life. This union was to be so complete that the two of them became an indivisible whole, never to be separated (Matthew 19:4-6). In God's mathematics, one plus one equals one.

Back come the Pharisees wanting to know why it was, then, that Moses allowed divorce to take place, if God's intention was that husband and wife should never be separated (7). This time, Jesus does reply directly to the question. They were not to mistake allowance for approval: it was a concession granted ' "because your hearts were hard. But it was not this way from the beginning" ' (8). When sin entered the heart of mankind, divorce may have become inevitable, but that didn't make it either good or desirable in God's sight.

Moses established laws to regulate divorce and to protect its victims, particularly women, who would often find themselves in vulnerable positions due to the culture of those times. The 'certificate of divorce' mentioned by the Pharisees (7) and by Jesus (5:31) was brought in by Moses to make the husband think much more carefully about divorcing his wife than he had needed to do before. Up until then, he could just simply throw her out on a mere whim. Thus, the original purpose behind this written letter of dismissal was to create an opportunity for people to think again before divorcing, in the hope that a reconciliation might be achieved, and the marriage preserved. Unfortunately, this appears to have rarely been the case, and divorce had become easier down the years from Moses to Jesus.

The only exception

Unlike the Pharisees, Jesus took the whole matter of divorce very seriously indeed. It is clear that Jesus does not want divorce to happen at all, preferring to see forgiveness and reconciliation take place between husband and wife, so they may remain 'one flesh' and their relationship be fully restored.

Jesus explains that to divorce and then to remarry, which is what usually happens, means that the husband is committing adultery, because in God's eyes he is still 'one flesh' with his previous wife (9). Not only that, but the wife whom he has divorced is then put in the position by her ex-husband of committing adultery with the man she marries next, thus making him an adulterer too (5:32). Another fact to bear in mind is that Jesus is also targeting those who were deliberately using the provision for divorce to indulge their lust for others, thus abusing the sacredness and life-long commitment of marriage.

But in spite of the fact that divorce is anathema to Jesus, He does actually allow it for one reason, and for one reason only: and that is because of 'marital unfaithfulness' (19:9; 5:32). The word in the original Greek is *porneia*, which means physical sexual immorality. This was the main cause of marital breakdown and subsequent divorce then, and it still is today. That is why the Bible speaks so strongly against sexual immorality. But even if this has taken place, divorce doesn't have to be the result. As mentioned before, God would prefer to see forgiveness, reconciliation and restoration take place.

Key words

'Marriages are made in heaven' is a well-known maxim, but

marriage needs to be worked *out* on earth, and on a daily basis at that! As in any relationship, there will be arguments and differences of opinion. Some will be trivial, others serious. But as we have made our vows before God, our intentions should always be to keep them, and to work to that end with determination and vigour. Divorce should never enter our minds.

In my experience, many couples try to hide the fact that they are having problems, because they are under the misapprehension that this means their marriages are failing. Nothing could be further from the truth. All marriages have their difficult times, and, in my experience, to admit there are problems is the first step to dealing with them. Too often these days it seems that divorce is the first and only step in the thinking of a lot of people, rather than a last resort.

Now, I am no marriage guidance counsellor, but in seeking to help Christian couples down the years I have come back to those three key words of forgiveness, reconciliation (which more often than not involves compromise) and restoration time and again. If there is the desire for these on both sides, and the willingness to put them into practice, then there is every chance that the marriage will not only be saved but strengthened and deepened. Jesus' teaching clearly shows that this is what God expects of members of His Kingdom who find themselves in such situations.

Hard questions

However, we all know that there are times when Christian marriages do break down and end in separation or divorce. Sexual unfaithfulness is still the primary cause of this, and, as we have seen, the teaching of Jesus clearly indicates that divorce is acceptable in that situation.

But what about all the other awful situations which can arise that bring the marriage to the point of breakdown? After every attempt at reconciliation and restoration has failed, is divorce permissible in those situations too? For example, if a wife is being subjected to abuse, or cruelty, or violence, can it be wrong for her to leave her husband? Some would say that separation is the better course, but apparently such an option was unknown in Jesus' day. You were single, married or divorced. This would seem to make separation the same as divorce as far as Jesus' teaching is concerned.

And then there is the question of remarriage. Are all those who have been involved in divorce, even those who are clearly the 'injured parties', to be condemned to lives of loneliness, since to remarry would mean committing adultery? I have nothing but admiration for people in this position who still consider themselves to be married to their spouses, even though separation or divorce has taken place, and have therefore decided not to remarry. This is despite the fact that they were the 'injured parties', and their spouses may have remarried. But equally, I find myself supporting people who were the 'injured parties' and who have decided to remarry after their divorce.

These are the sorts of hard questions that all those involved in church leadership will have to face up to at some time or another. Before I found myself in such a position, I have to confess to being very hard-line and quite judgemental in these matters. However, after actually meeting and coming to love many people down the years whose hearts have been broken and whose lives have been scarred by such situations, I quickly came to realise that each case is complex, and has to be treated both sympathetically and on its own merits. Of course we must apply Jesus' teaching, but surely we must do so with compassion, seeking God's guidance and wisdom on each specific case. After all, He is first and foremost a God of compassion.

How we need to support in prayer both our brothers and sisters who are going through the agony and trauma of a marriage that is falling apart, and those who are trying to pick up the pieces of their lives after a marriage relationship has irrevocably ended. And how we need to pray for wisdom and insight for all those who are involved in marriage counselling, as they seek to minister to those in traumatic situations.

4) Vows, Dishonesty, and Truthfulness (33-37)

The statement that Jesus makes on this occasion is not actually a quotation of any of the laws of Moses (33). Rather, it is a summary of various quotations to do with the keeping of oaths, which presumably had been used by the rabbis down the years.

Making and breaking

A person would swear an oath, asking God to witness his vow, and to punish him if he didn't keep it. In practice, vows were frequently taken lightly and casually, often with no intention on the part of the maker of the vow of keeping them. Such false swearing is condemned by the third commandment, which states: 'You shall not misuse the name of the Lord your God, for the Lord will not hold anyone guiltless who misuses his name' (Exodus 20:7). This warning is reflected elsewhere in the Law: ' "Do not swear falsely by my name and so profane the name of your God" ' (Leviticus 19:12). Failure to keep an oath sworn in

God's name means that God's name is dishonoured as a result. To make a vow and then to break it is clearly forbidden: ' "When a man makes a vow to the Lord or takes an oath to obligate himself by a pledge, he must not break his word but must do everything he said" ' (Numbers 30:2).

Not surprisingly, the Pharisees had sought to find ways around these severe prohibitions. They were teaching that what these laws actually meant was that only vows sworn using God's name were binding: oaths sworn in other ways were not so binding. Jesus took them to task about this on another occasion, exposing the stupidity of this reasoning (Matthew 23:16-22). All vows were to be honoured, no matter what they had been sworn by.

And that is the point Jesus is making here (34-36). To separate vows sworn by God and those not so sworn is ridiculous, because everything in the world relates to God in some way. Even our own heads were designed and created by God: we can't even stop our natural hair colour changing.

The heart of the problem

Jesus actually tells His followers not to swear oaths at all (34a). They should be totally unnecessary. The fact that oaths and vows are necessary is a mark of the dishonesty and untruthfulness that permeates human society. This is the heart of the problem. An example of this is to be found in what happens in a court of law. There, witnesses are asked to affirm that they are telling the truth by swearing an oath to that effect.

Another example of our tendency to be dishonest and untruthful is clearly seen in what we say to one another. How many times do we hear people come out with sentences such as: 'I'm telling the truth, honestly I am! I'm not kidding, I really am! I promise! You've got to believe me!' If everyone told the truth all the time, such assurances would not be necessary. In view of all this, it is interesting that the Jews themselves have a proverb which says: 'He who tells the truth saves himself the trouble of swearing.'

One in a thousand

Truth builds trust. If we know we can always and without exception rely on the word of someone, what a difference that makes to our relationship with him. Jesus expects us to be such people: ' "Simply let your 'Yes' be 'Yes' and your 'No' be 'No' " '(37a). People whose word can be trusted without fail: people who are characterised by their truthfulness.

This isn't easy when those around us are lying to their advantage, and manipulating – or being 'economical' with – the truth for their own selfish ends. As William Shakespeare wrote: 'To be honest as this world goes, is to be one man picked out of a thousand.' But as we keep on seeing, to be members of God's Kingdom means adopting whole different attitudes and lifestyles which mark us out from the world. As the apostle Paul writes: 'Therefore each of you must put off falsehood and speak truthfully' (Ephesians 4:25a). The challenge to us is this: are we known as people who are honest, keep our word, and tell the truth?

Seriously serious

Interestingly, James quotes these words of Jesus at the very point in his epistle where his readers would have been expecting an oath to confirm that all he had written was true. This was the accepted custom and practice in a Greek letter. Instead, he takes this most appropriate opportunity to remind his readers of

Jesus' teaching about the use of oaths and His command that we tell the truth, adding the warning that failure to do so means that 'you will be condemned' (James 5:12). Always being truthful is a serious matter, and seriously matters as far as God is concerned. As John Calvin said: 'Nothing is deemed more precious by God than truth.'

5) Retaliation, Revenge, and Response (38-42)

In the Law of Moses we read these words: "But if there is serious injury, you are to take life for life, eye for eye, tooth for tooth, hand for hand, foot for foot, burn for burn, wound for wound, bruise for bruise" ' (Exodus 21:23-25). Jesus refers to this statement (38), and then moves on to tackle the issues it raises.

The law of talion
This law of talion, as it is called, covered both the punishment for the offender and the compensation for the victim. The principle it laid down was that both punishment and compensation were to match the crime exactly, and not exceed it. This was a significant advance on what was happening at the time in surrounding countries, where punishments often did exceed crimes in the most cruel and barbaric ways. It also limited the compensation that a victim could receive.

The law was a statement of principle, and was not expected to be taken literally, with eyes being gouged out, teeth being knocked out, and so on. Indeed, there is no evidence to suggest that it was ever enforced literally. Certainly, by the time of Jesus the payment of damages had become the norm.

It is also important to understand that this statement of principle was only ever intended as a guide for judges in the law courts. It was a part of the civil law, not the moral law. There was never any intention that it should apply to the area of personal relationships, and it was certainly not to be used to justify taking the law into their own hands, as Pharisees of the school of Shammai maintained. Indeed, this was expressly forbidden: ' "Do not seek revenge or bear a grudge against one of your people" ' (Leviticus 19:18a). Such problems were to be sorted out in a court of law and nowhere else.

Settling the score

Someone once said, 'Don't get mad: get even!' And if we are honest, this is often our first reaction when we are treated wrongly by someone. We bristle at the thought that somebody might have got one over on us, and we set out to settle the score. How many times do we hear people saying words to the effect that they were just paying somebody back for what they had done to them?

But Jesus has some tough things to say to us on this score. He begins by stating: '"But I tell you, Do not resist an evil person"' (39a). The actual meaning of these words has been the subject of much debate. However, it seems to me that the Good News Bible translation more accurately reflects the whole of the teaching of Jesus on this subject when it renders this sentence: '"Do not take revenge on someone who wrongs you"'. He expects us to respond with gentleness, love and generosity of spirit at all times and in all situations, even when we are unjustly treated. However, this doesn't mean that we are not to resist evil or the devil. Indeed, there are many Scriptures which encourage us to do precisely that (Ephesians 6:13; James 4:7; 1 Peter 5:8, 9).

Jesus then goes on to use three examples which teach us not to retaliate or seek revenge against anyone, even where to do so would be within our civil rights. And we are certainly not to take the law into our own hands.

Rights and wrongs

All the three examples Jesus uses involve unjust treatment which violates an individual's civil and human rights. On each occasion, the victim would be within his rights to seek redress. But that would be to return the evil of retaliation for the evil of the deed. Jesus is saying that whenever we are faced with such evil, we must respond with good. As the apostle Paul would write years later, quite possibly with these very examples in mind: 'Do not repay anyone evil for evil. . . . Do not take revenge, my friends. . . . Do not be overcome by evil, but overcome evil with good' (Romans 12:17a, 19a, 21).

Jesus expects us to respond in a different way; in a costly way; in a way which would be totally unexpected by the perpetrator of the assault; in a way that is completely foreign to the kingdoms of this world. We are not to insist on our rights, even when we would be perfectly justified in so doing. Such an attitude is so totally contrary to the society in which we live, where everyone seems to know his rights, and to demand them with increasing fervour. Whether he knows his responsibilities and pursues them with equal vigour is quite another matter.

Alfred Plummer assesses the various courses of action open to us thus: 'To return evil for good is devilish; to return good for good is human; to return good for evil is divine.'

1) Turn

Jesus sets out His scenarios as follows. Firstly, ' "If someone strikes you on the right cheek, turn to him the other also" ' (39b). In the Middle East, a slap on the right cheek with the back of the hand is a grave insult; an action which, if taken to court, could result in a hefty fine for the perpetrator. To slap the person back would be the reaction of most people, but Jesus teaches His followers in these dramatic words that they are not to retaliate in kind, nor resort to taking the perpetrator to court to gain redress, but rather to allow him to continue to insult them as much as he likes.

Appropriate

There may well be occasions when this is personally required of us, quite literally: and such a response would be appropriate in those circumstances. Jesus Himself refused to retaliate when faced with such actual provocation and violence (Isaiah 50:6; Mark 14:65, 15:16-20; 1 Peter 2:21-23). The same is true of Martin Luther King Jun., who worked tirelessly to promote the cause of civil rights for all black people in the United States of America until his assassination in 1968. In the course of this struggle, he was subjected to unprovoked violence on countless occasions, yet he never retaliated. On one occasion he simply said: 'Returning violence for violence multiplies violence, adding deeper darkness to a night already devoid of stars.' He always urged his followers to 'meet hate with love.'

But I believe that we need to keep a sense of balance here. Jesus was fulfilling His mission and fulfilling the prophecies which spoke of what would happen to the Suffering Servant of God. Martin Luther King believed he had been given a special mission by God, who gave him great strength and wisdom to carry it out in the most effective way possible in the situation in which he found himself, which was to use the strategy of non-violence as a political weapon.

Inappropriate

However, it seems to me that it would be both dangerous and unwise to apply this principle of turning the other cheek literally on all occasions; and I don't think that Jesus expects us to. He was illustrating the principle He was teaching: returning good for evil, making the right response, showing the right attitude, and not seeking revenge. Jesus is not saying that evil, cruelty and injustice must be suffered without protest; rather, He is saying that violence will achieve nothing.

Indeed, there are certain settings and situations in which to turn the other cheek would be inappropriate: for example, when being bullied, mugged, or sexually abused. It is inconceivable that Jesus would expect us to allow such acts to happen without our attempting to restrain the perpetrators. While retaliation or seeking revenge would always be the wrong response, it seems to me that the principle of restraining attackers is perfectly compatible with Jesus' teaching in the gospels. Not to do so would be a charter for every bully, thug and abuser to perpetrate his despicable acts of violence towards the vulnerable in society.

I write about this with some feeling, as I was bullied for a short time when a young child because I refused to hit back when attacked, having been taught that Jesus expected us to turn the other cheek. To defend oneself against the bully is to my mind perfectly justifiable, whereas beating him to a pulp, or getting one's friends to attack him would not be. It could be argued that by restraining the bully you are in fact acting gently towards him, and showing him a loving attitude. By your actions, you are teaching him something he needs to learn so that he can develop as a socially acceptable individual: namely, that he shouldn't go round attacking others. And this applies equally to all perpetrators of violence or evil of any kind.

Unlike the practice in the world around us, the aim of our conduct and response when faced with such situations is not to get one over, but to win one over. As James Dobson said: 'There is no greater opportunity to influence our fellow-man for Christ than to respond with love when we have been unmistakably wronged.'

Someone once said: 'There is nothing stronger than gentleness.' The apostle Paul tells us: 'The fruit of the Spirit is love . . . gentleness and self-control' (Galatians 5:22, 23). To refrain from retaliation in favour of gentleness and to control the desire for revenge show a strength which comes from love; and this is the response which God expects to see in each one of us.

2) Give

Jesus' second example is: ' "And if someone wants to sue you and take your tunic, let him have your cloak as well" ' (40). The tunic was an undergarment, whereas the cloak was worn on top, and it was a protected garment under the Law of Moses: ' "If you take your neighbour's cloak as a pledge, return it to him by sunset, because his cloak is the only covering he has for his body. What else will he sleep in?" ' (Exodus 22:26, 27a).

Although the reason for this law had long passed, because most people had roofs over their heads by then, Jesus deliberately used it as an example to show that a person's response should be that of going to great lengths involving personal cost to return good for evil, even when he has been treated unfairly.

To give when it hurts is the costly, but a loving and appropriate response that is required of us.

3) Go

Thirdly, Jesus says: ' "If someone forces you to go one mile, go with him two miles" ' (41). The Roman soldier was within his rights to make a civilian carry his pack or some other article for no more than a mile, or demand the use of his donkey for a similar purpose. We see this when Jesus collapses while carrying His cross, and a soldier forces Simon of Cyrene to carry it for Him (Matthew 27:32; Mark 15:21; Luke 23:26).

In this example, Jesus is teaching us to do more than what is required of us. We are even to allow people to take advantage of us as we seek to return good for evil. Once again, we are to respond with costly love. We are to go when it hurts. As someone said: 'Go the extra mile, which is one stretch of highway where there are never any traffic jams.'

4) Do

Jesus now presents a fourth scenario which is completely different from the three that have gone before. This one does not involve unjust treatment at the hands of someone imposing himself upon us. Rather, it is an opportunity for us to apply the same principles in situations where we are not under duress: ' "Give to the one who asks you, and do not turn away from the one who wants to borrow from you" ' (42). Luke records Jesus as saying: ' "Give to everyone who asks you, and if anyone takes what belongs to you, do not demand it back" ' (6:30).

Jesus is, in effect, telling us to give to others with love and generosity, not seeking revenge if they don't pay up. So, this scenario crystallises all that has been taught in the three previous examples concerning the right attitude and the right response. The challenge is to do it. And we never know what may result as a consequence of showing such a spirit of love and generosity to others, as the following story illustrates.

The pianist and the politician

Many years ago two young men were working their way through Stanford University in the United States of America. At one point their money was almost gone; so they decided to engage the great Polish pianist Paderewski for a concert and use the profits for board and tuition. Paderewski's manager asked for a guarantee of $2,000. The students worked hard to promote the concert, but they were $400 short.

After the performance, they went to the musician, offering him all the money they had raised, and promising to pay the $400 as soon as they could. It appeared that their college days were over. 'No, boys, that won't do,' said the pianist. 'Take all your expenses out of this $1,600, and keep for each of you ten per cent of the balance for your work. Then let me have the rest.'

Years passed. Paderewski became premier of Poland following World War I. Thousands of his countrymen were starving. Only one man could help: the head of the U.S. Food and Relief Bureau. Paderewski's appeal to him brought thousands of tons of food. Later he met the American statesman to thank him. 'That's all right,' replied Herbert Hoover. 'Besides, you don't remember, but you helped me when I was a student.'

6. Neighbours, Enemies, and Love (43-48)

Not only did the law forbid revenge: it also commanded the Jew to love his neighbour. In fact, there is an occasion in the Law when these two stipulations are presented together in one verse, the first part of which we have already noted. The full verse reads: ' "Do not seek revenge or bear a grudge against one of your people, but love your neighbour as yourself" ' (Leviticus 19:18).

Addition and subtraction

Having dealt with the prohibition contained in the first part of this verse, Jesus now focuses on the command laid down in the second part. What He quotes is not the law itself, but what the Pharisees were teaching (43). Their interpretation of what the law said shows two significant differences from what it actually stated. There was an addition, and a subtraction.

First came the subtraction: they omitted the clause 'as yourself'. The effect of this was to reduce the standard of love required from the high value it had been set at, to what each individual would consider to be reasonable, given the particular 'neighbour' involved. That meant it would vary considerably!

Second came the addition: they inserted the phrase 'and hate your enemy'. The Pharisees claimed that the context in which this command was given was such that they were obliged to love only those who loved them in return, and only those who were fellow Jews at that (see Leviticus 19). They had then gone on to infer from various other Scriptures, such as Deuteronomy 23:3-6 and Psalm 139:19-22, that they should hate their enemies. They conveniently ignored other Scriptures which commanded them to do good to their enemies, for instance, Exodus 23:4, 5 and Deuteronomy 22:1-4, which, taken together, clearly show that the same response was required in a case like this for both enemy and brother alike.

The meaning of loving

Once again, Jesus had something totally mind-blowing to tell them: ' "Love your enemies and pray for those who persecute you" ' (44). The concept of an enemy being a neighbour, and just as entitled to receive love as was their brother, must have left His disciples gasping and given the Pharisees apoplexy when they heard it. Jesus illustrated and emphasised this principle further on another occasion by telling the parable of the Good Samaritan. This parable makes it abundantly clear that our neighbour is anyone who is in need, and this qualifies him to receive our love. His race, colour, religion, and social status are irrelevant, as is whether he be friend or enemy. As Oswald Chambers said: 'If my heart is right with God, every human being is my neighbour.'

Luke records Jesus' teaching on this subject in slightly more detail: ' "Love your enemies, do good to those who hate you, bless those who curse you, pray for those who ill-treat you" ' (6:27, 28). At the very time when Luke and Matthew were recording these words of Jesus about how they should treat enemies and respond to mistreatment, the first Christians were suffering sustained persecution. These words were therefore very relevant to the times in which they were living; and they still are to the 250 million or so Christians across the world who are daily suffering persecution at the hands of various governments, dictatorships and authorities. Of these, 160,000 are martyred on average each year.

• Doing

Although most of us will not suffer such overt persecution, we are certainly all going to encounter hostility in various forms because of our witness to the Gospel and our allegiance to

Christ. In Luke 6:27, 28 we can clearly see three commands, which help us to clarify the forms which love for our enemies should take.

Firstly, loving involves doing: it is active, not passive. Jesus expects us to do good to our enemies. In the book of Proverbs we read: 'If your enemy is hungry, give him food to eat; if he is thirsty, give him water to drink. . . . and the Lord will reward you' (25:21, 22). This is another example of a Scripture conveniently ignored by the Pharisees.

One of the best illustrations I know of this being put into practice took place during the Second World War. It was the occasion when many of the British prisoners shared their rations and water with badly-wounded Japanese soldiers, and bandaged their wounds. When a furious British officer challenged them, one of the soldiers, Ernest Gordon, reminded him of the parable of the Good Samaritan. The officer replied that this was a different situation altogether, and that these Japanese soldiers were the enemy. It was then that Ernest remembered the words of Jesus: ' "But I tell you who hear me: Love your enemies, do good to those who hate you." '

• Blessing

Secondly, loving involves blessing. Instead of returning curse for curse, we are to do the exact opposite: to pray God's blessing upon those who wish us harm, and seek to bring blessing into their lives.

Another incident from World War II serves as a good illustration of this. A young American soldier was going off to fight against the Japanese. As his father put him on the train and waved goodbye, he turned with bitter tears and said, 'If my son is killed, I hope every Jap in the world is killed!' Yet the fact that the father was a Christian made it difficult to feel that way in reality. After a fierce struggle with himself, he finally realised that it was not Christian to hate, whether his son lived or died. He declared rather, 'I will not hate. I refuse to be destroyed by hate!' A year later the son was killed. Soon after, the life insurance money arrived. The father did not really need the ten thousand dollars; so he sent it to the Southern Baptist Foreign Mission Board and designated it for missions to the Japanese.

• Praying

Thirdly, loving involves praying: not for myself, that I might escape the wrath of my enemy; but rather interceding with God out of love on behalf of the one who *is* my enemy. Dietrich Bonhoeffer, who suffered at the hands of the Nazis in Buchenwald concentration camp, wrote: 'This is the supreme command. Through the medium of prayer we go to our enemy, stand by his side, and plead for him to God.' Jesus Himself is the supreme example of this, when He prays for those who are crucifying Him: 'Father, forgive them, for they do not know what they are doing' (Luke 23:34). And we are to follow His example.

T. E. McCully's son, Ed, was one of a group of missionaries killed by Auca Indians in Ecuador. Shortly after this incident, his father prayed these words: 'Lord, let me live long enough to see those fellows saved who killed our boys, that I may throw my arms around them and tell them I love them, because they love my Christ.' We can only imagine what it must have cost him to pray that prayer.

Dimitry's encounter

Once again we are seeing how God expects us as members of

His Kingdom to react and respond in a way which is different from that to be found in the kingdoms of the world; in a way that is costly to us and is unexpected by them; in a way which shows our distinctiveness from the world; in a way that shows God's love to the world. And, once again, God is not asking us to do something which He Himself has not done. The apostle Paul reminds us that Jesus died so that we could be reconciled to God 'when we were God's enemies' (Romans 5:10).

Dimitry Mustafin knows how difficult it is to love his enemies. He is a Russian scientist and university lecturer who once studied methods of attacking the West. Through the work of 'Gideons International' he became a Christian, and eventually joined that organisation. At a special celebration he was introduced to a man who had been an executioner for thirty years in the prison where many of Dimitry's relatives had been put to death. Dimitry says of this encounter: 'I wasn't able to look at his face because I saw the face of my grandfather. I wasn't able to speak with him because a lot of swear words were running into my mouth. I wasn't able to shake his hand, I was afraid that I would beat him. I was praying to the Lord and I asked the Lord to put love into my heart towards this man whom I hated so much.'

God answered Dimitry's prayer, to the extent that he spoke with this man, who already knew he was a terrible sinner, and led him to Christ. Dimitry continues: 'When we finished our prayer I looked into his eyes and I saw that they were wet. Then he shook my hand and we hugged each other. . . . It is still very difficult for me to understand, but it was a great lesson for me. I am very thankful that the Lord had chosen me as his instrument for bringing this man to the Lord. It is very easy to love good people, but it is so difficult to love our enemies . . . . But this is what our Lord is asking us to do.'

Missile alert

There is another aspect to this. God doesn't command us to love our enemies just for *their* benefit, but for *our* own benefit as well, lest we destroy ourselves by harbouring hostility towards others.

During the Second World War, the U.S. submarine *Tang* surfaced under the cover of darkness to fire on a large Japanese convoy off the coast of China. Since previous raids had left the American vessel with only eight torpedoes, the accuracy of every shot was absolutely essential. The first seven missiles were right on target; but when the eighth was launched, it suddenly deviated and headed right back at their own ship. The emergency alarm to submerge rang out, but it was too late. Within a matter of seconds, the U.S. sub received a direct hit and sank almost instantly.

As with unforgiveness, bitterness and resentment, the person who really suffers from feelings of hostility and enmity towards someone is me. These are all missiles of self-destruction which will render us at best disabled, and at worst totally unusable, in the service of the Master.

'Sons of your father'

We can all identify with the struggle which Dimitry experienced, although it is unlikely to be as intense as that for us. Yet Jesus told us that to love our enemies is to be 'sons of your Father in heaven' (45a). Such an attitude is a mark or a demonstration to the world that we are children of God. Interestingly, the only other occasion in the Sermon on the Mount when Jesus talks about our being sons of God is when we are peacemakers

(5:9), an illustration which is also connected with hostility.

After all, Jesus reminds us, this is the way that God loves. In the matter of provision for His creation, He does not discriminate between those who love Him and those who don't; between those who are His children and those who are His enemies; between those who obey His commands and those who disobey them. Not at all. He loves everyone, so: ' "He causes his sun to rise on the evil and the good, and sends rain on the righteous and the unrighteous" ' (45b). And it is such perfect love that we are to emulate (48). This is God's standard for us and His challenge to us. And He expects us to strive to fulfil this high ideal, even though we may never fully achieve it in our lives.

Something extra

According to Jesus, to love those who also love us is to be expected, and brings us no credit at all. Even 'tax collectors', who had no moral scruples whatever as they lined their own pockets, and 'pagans', who were a byword for ungodly behaviour, did that (46, 47). The question Jesus asks us is: ' "What are you doing more than others?" ' (47).

That something extra which God expects to see in us is perfect love: a love that transcends all boundaries and breaks down all barriers; a love which reaches out to all people, not just to those who reach out to us; a love that encompasses even our enemies.

A young girl once heard a preacher talking about the subject of loving our enemies, and was obviously very keen to put this principle into practice in her life. But she had a problem, as she explained to the preacher in her note: 'Dear Preacher, I heard you say to love our enemies. I am only six and do not have any yet. I hope to have some when I am seven. Your friend, Love, Amy.'

The law of love

Our attitudes are to be governed by the law of love. Jesus did not say we are to like our enemies; we are to love them. We are bound to dislike those who are our enemies. Yet it is possible to love them through the work of God's grace in our lives and the empowering of the Holy Spirit within us, enabling us to love in a supernatural way; enabling us truly to love our enemies.

The same principle applies to our dealings with people whom we may not class as enemies, yet we find it difficult to like. We may meet them at work, through recreational activities, through our church outreach programmes, or even, dare I say it, in the membership of our church! May God so work in us by His grace and empower us by His Spirit that we are able to overcome our natural dislikes and to love as God loves: unconditionally and unreservedly; selflessly and unselfishly; inclusively and constructively; ceaselessly and unfailingly.

Tough stuff

It is at this point in Jesus' teaching that Luke includes what has become known as 'The Golden Rule': ' "Do to others as you would have them do to you" ' (6:31). This is a one-sentence summary of the teaching contained in Luke 6:27-30, which is the equivalent of Matthew 5:38-48. In Matthew's account, this command appears later in the Sermon on the Mount, and is completed with the words ' "for this sums up the Law and the Prophets" ' (7:12). God expects us to treat others as we would like to be treated. And if we do that, we shall automatically be fulfilling all that God requires of us in our daily living.

So, whenever we find ourselves in situations where we are unsure how to act, this rule provides all the guidance we need. Some Christians find it more helpful to think about how Jesus Himself might act when faced with such dilemmas, and have taken to wearing items inscribed 'WWJD?': What Would Jesus Do?

This 'Golden Rule' is to be found in other religions and philosophies, but always in a negative form rather than the positive instruction which Jesus uses. For example, Confucius is said to have taught: 'Do not to others what you would not wish done to yourself'; Rabbi Hillel said: 'Do not do to others what is hateful to you.'

I once heard this statement parodied as 'Do to others *before* they do to you', which for me sums up the difference in attitude between those who are of the kingdom of the world and those who belong to the Kingdom of God. Or it should do! However, there are occasions when we all fail in this respect. And no wonder: these last two sections (38-48) contain teaching which is arguably the toughest in the whole of the Sermon on the Mount. John Stott is in no doubt of this. He wrote: 'Nowhere is the challenge of the Sermon greater. Nowhere is the distinctness of the Christian counter-culture more obvious. Nowhere is our need of the power of the Holy Spirit (whose first fruit is love) more compelling.'

May God so fill us daily with His power and love that we shall be able to rise to the challenge of these teachings, to put them into practice in our lives, and thus be distinct from the world around us.

Questions for group study

Matthew 5:17-48; 7:12

Verses 17-20

Discuss
1 Why did Jesus need to state that He had not come to abolish the Law or the Prophets (17)?

Background
2 Which part of the Jewish Scriptures was covered by the term 'the Law'?
3 The laws themselves were divided into three sections. What were they, and what matters did each one of them deal with?
4 Which part of the Jewish Scriptures was covered by the term 'the Prophets'?

Discuss
5 Why does Matthew record what Jesus has to say about the Law and the Prophets, whereas Mark and Luke pay far less attention to these matters?
6 With regard to the Law, how do we know that Jesus was a loyalist rather than an abolitionist?
7 In what two particular ways did Jesus fulfil the Law and the Prophets?
8 In this regard, why is the Transfiguration such a signifcant event?
9 How do Jesus' illustrations of the patch and the wineskins help to explain what was happening?
(See Matthew 9:16, 17; Mark 2:21, 22; Luke 5:36-39).

10 In what respect are the ceremonial, civil and moral laws given to Moses binding on us today?
11 Why did the righteousness of the Pharisees fall short of what God is looking for?

Apply
12 What would be evidence of a righteousness of heart?
13 How can we possibly achieve this?

Verses 21-26
Discuss
14 Why does Jesus now go on to give examples of this deeper righteousness?
15 What did the Pharisees believe and teach about the sixth Commandment?
16 What kind of anger is Jesus talking about?

Background
17 What expressions of anger did the Pharisees teach were unacceptable?
18 Why according to Jesus was calling someone 'you fool' the ultimate expression of anger?

Apply
19 What lessons about dealing with anger can we learn from the story of Cain (Genesis 4:3-12)?
20 If we have allowed anger to take root within us, what three steps do we need to take?

21 Why do we need to be reconciled with someone before coming to worship God?
22 What can be the consequences for us of not being reconciled to others?
23 Why is it often difficult to be reconciled with others?
24 Why are we so much better at listing offences done against us, rather than being aware of the distress we may have caused to others?

Verses 27-30
Discuss
25 Why is it reasonable to assume that Jesus is talking about all forms of sexual immorality in this section?
26 How do we know that the desire for a physical relationship with the opposite sex is a good drive?
27 Why has the prevailing attitude to sex in the Western world moved far away from God's original intention?
28 What does Jesus say is the only way to deal with lust?
29 In what ways is lust stimulated in the media and in society?

Apply
30 What advice would you give to a teenage daughter about the way she should dress?

Discuss
31 Why does Jesus say that having the desire to commit the act is as wrong as the act itself (28)?
32 What is the only way to stop this adultery of the heart?

Apply

33 What are some of the danger signs that show lust is developing?

34 Should we fall prey to lustful desires, what steps do we need to take?

Discuss

35 Why is sex outside of marriage to be avoided?

36 What dramatic picture does Jesus use to impress upon us how vital self-control and self-discipline are in sexual matters?

Apply

37 What is Jesus actually expecting us to do in our lives to prevent us falling prey to lust?

38 What advice would you give to a teenage Christian who is being pressurised to conform to the prevailing culture?

Discuss

39 Why does Jesus speak in such a strong way on this subject?

Verses 31, 32 [also Matthew 19:3-9]
Background

40 What were the two schools of thought within the Jewish religion on the subject of divorce?

Discuss
41 Why did Jesus not answer the Pharisees' question directly?
42 What does Jesus have to say about marriage (19:3-6)?

Background
43 Why was divorce allowed by Moses?
44 Why had the 'certificate of divorce' been brought in?

Discuss
45 How does divorce result in adultery being committed?
46 What sort of person was Jesus particularly targeting when He said this?
47 What is the only ground for divorce allowed by Jesus?

Apply
48 How is it best to go about resolving any problems in a marriage?
49 What in particular does God expect Christian couples to be willing to do in order that their marriage relationship might be restored?

Discuss
50 As the leader of a church, how would you deal with the following situations in your congregation:
* A woman who wants to divorce her violent and abusive husband.
* A man whose wife left him, who now wants to remarry in the church.

* A man who wants to marry, in the church, the woman whom he left his wife to be with.
* Any other situations that are known to the group.
51 Is there a case for applying the teaching of Jesus with compassion, or should we always maintain a strict interpretation?

Verses 33-37
Background
52 What was the teaching of the Law with regard to oaths and vows?
53 What usually happened in practice?
54 What were the Pharisees teaching?

Discuss
55 What did Jesus have to say on this subject?
56 What does the fact that oaths and vows are found to be necessary in society indicate?

Apply
57 In this regard, what does God expect of us?
58 In which areas do we find it most difficult to be honest and truthful all the time?
59 Why is hard to maintain such standards?

Discuss
60 Why is being truthful fundamental to building successful relationships?

Verses 38-42

Background

61 What principle did the law of talion lay down?
62 How were Pharisees of the school of Shammai misusing this law?

Discuss

63 What is the probable meaning of the command: 'Do not resist an evil person' ?
64 Does this mean that we should not resist evil? (See Ephesians 6:13; James 4:7; 1 Peter 5:8, 9).
65 What do the three examples Jesus uses have in common?

Apply

66 How does God expect us to respond when we are badly treated? (See also Romans 12:17a, 19a, 21).
67 Why is this a costly way to respond?

Discuss

68 What is Jesus teaching by means of His first scenario?

Apply

69 On what occasions might this literally be the most appropriate reaction?
70 In what sorts of situations might it be dangerous, unwise or inappropriate to apply the principle literally? Why?
71 What might be the most appropriate response in such circumstances?

72 How is gentleness a sign of strength?

Background
73 What Jewish law did Jesus have in mind as He presented the second scenario?
74 Which right of the Roman soldier did Jesus use in the third scenario?

Discuss
75 What is Jesus teaching by means of these two scenarios?

Apply
76 In what situations have members of the group been, which have demanded such responses as outlined in these two scenarios?

Discuss
77 How does the fourth scenario differ from the previous three?
78 How does it crystallise all that Jesus has taught by means of the other scenarios?

Verses 43-48
Background
79 Besides forbidding revenge, what did the Law also command the Jew to do? (See Leviticus 19:18).
80 What two significant differences from what the law said were to be found in the way the Pharisees interpreted it?

Discuss

81 Why would the concept of loving and praying for your enemies have been anathema to the Pharisees?

Background

82 What was happening at the time when these words were being recorded which made them especially relevant?

Apply

83 What are we doing as individuals and in our church to support our brothers and sisters in Christ who are being persecuted daily for their faith?

Discuss

84 According to Luke 6:27, 28, what three forms should love for our enemies take?

Apply

85 What can we learn from the actions of Ernest Gordon and his fellow prisoners; the response of the father of the American soldier killed by the Japanese; the prayer of T. E. McCully?

86 What danger is there for us personally if we harbour hostility towards others?

Discuss

87 How is the fact that we love our enemies a mark that we are children of God? (See verse 45).

Apply

88 What is that something extra which God expects to see in us (verses 47, 48)?
89 Is it possible to love people without liking them?
90 How can we automatically fulfil all that God requires of us? (See Luke 6:31; Matthew 7:12).

For personal prayer and reflection

Is my daily walk characterised by a righteousness of heart?
Am I willing to be reconciled with those who have wronged me?
Am I being wise in my relationships with the opposite sex?
Am I honouring God or conforming to the sexual norms and attitudes of society?
Is there anyone who is having a difficult time in their marriage at the moment whom I could support?
Do I have the reputation of being honest and truthful at all times?
How do I respond when treated badly or unfairly?
What do I find most difficult about returning good for evil?
Do I love, seek to bless, and pray for those who are hostile to me?
Am I self-destructing due to hostility towards someone?
Do I treat others as I would like to be treated?

CHAPTER 4

Don't Be Like Them

Matthew 6:1-18

The secrecy test (1-6; 16-18)

'Be careful'

Having spoken about the social obligations of the law (5:21-48), Jesus now turns His attention to the prescribed religious duties: from the subject of moral righteousness to that of religious righteousness.

There were three religious duties: almsgiving (giving money to the poor), prayer and fasting; and it seems clear that Jesus expected His disciples, both then and now, to continue observing them. But when carrying out these religious 'acts of righteousness', they were to 'Be careful': careful that they were not observing them merely 'to be seen' by other people (1a). Jesus was challenging His disciples to consider their reasons for giving alms, for praying and for fasting. What were the motives behind their actions? Were they self-centred or God-centred? Were they done so that *they* were praised or God was praised? Were they done for men to see and approve, or for God to see and approve?

If the answer in each case was the former, then ' "you will have no reward from your Father in heaven" ' (1b). As C. H. Spurgeon put it: 'There is no reward from God to those who seek it from men.' Any such act which is done for the wrong reasons is vain, empty and meaningless in God's sight. But to those whose motives are pure and righteous, Jesus promises a reward (4b, 6b, 18b).

All for show

Having set out this important principle, Jesus then goes on to illustrate it by taking each of the religious duties in turn. In each case, He begins by exposing the hypocrisy and insincerity of people like the Pharisees. They zealously practised all these religious obligations, but for all the wrong reasons. In fact, they had but one motive in carrying them out: to win the praise and honour of those around them, while pretending to do them to bring honour to God (2a); and therein lay their hypocrisy. They wanted people to be impressed by and to comment on their religious devotion; so they made a public display of their fulfilment of these duties. They put on a show calculated to achieve the maximum effect.

Jesus uses vivid and amusing caricatures to portray their ostentatious behaviour. They trumpet their giving to the poor and needy; their times of prayer are performances of Oscar-winning proportions; and when fasting, they make a spectacle of themselves which any make-up artist would be proud of (2a, 5a, 16a).

The gasps of admiration at the apparent holiness of these men, and expressions of wonder at their devotion to their religious duties were music to the ears of the religious leaders. But the show they put on only showed them up for what they were. True, the needy still received money at their hands, notwithstanding the motive behind the giving of it, which I'm sure the poor didn't care about anyway.

But Jesus cared about it. He looked beyond what they did to why they did it, and pronounced that when they received the praise of men, they ' " received their reward in full" ' (2b, 5b, 16b). The Pharisees thought they were building up favour with God, but God was not impressed; in fact, quite the opposite. There would be no God-given reward for these Pharisees, or for any others who showed a similarly hypocritical attitude. All their 'acts of righteousness' were a complete waste of time as far as God was concerned.

Be different

Jesus not only exposes the hypocrisy of the religious leaders, but commands us not to be like them. As members of His Kingdom, we are to be different when we give, pray and fast (2a, 5a, 16a). And Jesus goes on to explain *how* we should be different:

- When we give money to the needy, it is to be kept so secret that even our left hand doesn't know what our right hand is doing (3, 4a), which means that other people won't be aware either.
- When we pray, we are commanded to '"go into your room, close the door and pray to your Father"' (6a). No one else is to know that we are at prayer. Interestingly, the word used for 'room' here refers to the storeroom of a

house in those days, which usually had no window and was the only one that could be locked. We are to shut ourselves off from everyone else, completely in secret, to the extent that no one can even see us or disturb us.
- When we fast, we are to adopt a normal appearance and attitude, so that our time of fasting will be a secret known only to our Father in heaven (17, 18a).

Jesus is not actually expecting us to hide our left hands behind our backs when we give with our right hands, or to lock ourselves away in darkened rooms in order to pray properly. But what He is expecting us to do is to make sure that our giving, our praying and our fasting are most secret matters, just between us and God; matters that no one else knows anything about. And that will ensure that our motives for doing them are pure and righteous.

A neglected discipline?

God expects us to minister to the needy, and to pray. But what about fasting? The Jews were required to fast at least once a year on the Day of Atonement (Leviticus 23:32). The Pharisees actually fasted twice a week, as the Pharisee in the parable was not slow to remind God (Luke 18:12a); but we know what their motive was for doing this.

Although we are no longer living under the religious obligations of the ceremonial law, it is clear that God still expects us to fast, usually so that we can spend more time in prayer and meditation. In my experience, that extra time spent in God's presence often serves to sharpen my spiritual awareness and to heighten my spiritual faculties, so that I become more conscious of God's presence and His leading in my life.

Fasting involves going without food; some would say

without liquid as well, for a period of time. Such physical self-denial is also a way of showing God, not to mention ourselves, that we really do mean business regarding the particular problems we are praying earnestly about at the moment. These may be personal matters. They may be to do with the church, such as what to do about a difficult situation, or whether to embark on a certain project. Fasting together as God's people often results in the way forward being made clear.

Of these three disciplines, fasting is the one that is probably the most neglected. And, in my opinion, 'disciplines' is an excellent word for them, because, if we are really honest, they are all activities which we have to discipline ourselves to do, simply on account of the fact that they are so demanding on our finances, resources, time and will-power.

Rewards

Jesus promises that our Father in heaven will reward us when we give to the needy, pray and fast for the right reasons. This reward is not so much something to be received in heaven, but experienced on earth.

As we give to the needy, so God rewards us by giving to us in all kinds of ways, thus enriching our lives (Luke 6:38). As we pray, the reward we receive is that of having our requests answered by our loving heavenly Father. As we fast, our reward is the experience of being drawn closer to God, and becoming more sensitive to His presence and leading in our lives. None of these blessings was experienced by the Pharisees.

The litmus test

One of the few things I do remember from the science lessons of my schooldays is that if I dip a piece of litmus paper in a chemical solution, it will turn red if it's acid and blue if it's alkali. The litmus test never fails to identify correctly the true nature of the substance. In the same way, the secrecy test never fails to identify the true nature of the substance of our motives.

If we're not prepared to give to the needy, to pray and to fast in secret, without anyone else knowing what we're doing, then there is absolutely no doubt that we are carrying out these actions for the wrong reasons. Which, if true, makes us just as hypocritical and insincere as the religious leaders of Jesus' day, and just as guilty of acts that are vain, empty and meaningless in the sight of the One whose name we claim to be seeking to honour.

Yet each of these areas does present its own temptations: to see our names on lists of donors to church causes or charities so that people will know how much we give and how generous we are; to be known as those who can lift whole congregations when they pray, or who spend much time in private prayer and study; to be regarded with a certain admiration as people who regularly fast and hear from God. It is with good reason that Jesus began His teaching on this subject with: 'Be careful' (1).

Going public

However, all this talk of secrecy doesn't mean that there is no place for giving publicly, for public prayer and for fasting together as God's people. The Early Church certainly did so (Acts 4:23-37; 11:27-30; 13:2, 3; 14:23). And in my experience, such times are blessed by God. But the same challenging questions still need to be answered by each one of us individually on these occasions, just as much as when we are acting on our own. Questions such as: What is my motive for doing this? Is it self-centred or God-centred? Is it to gain men's acclaim or

God's approval? If God asked me to do this in secret, would I?

In her poem entitled 'I Wonder', Ruth Harms Calkin considers her own response:

> 'You know, Lord, how I serve You
>> with great emotional fervour in the limelight.
>
> You know how eagerly I speak for You at a Women's Club.
> You know my genuine enthusiasm at a Bible study.
> But how would I react, I wonder,
>> if You pointed to a basin of water
>> and asked me to wash the calloused feet
>> of a bent and wrinkled old woman
>> day after day, month after month,
>> in a room where nobody saw and nobody knew?'

How to pray (7–15)

Let's now go back to the section on prayer to examine the extended teaching which Jesus gave on this subject. Here we see Jesus using the same technique we have already observed: first describing the wrong way, then setting out the right way. The vivid contrast between the two serves to make what God requires of us crystal clear.

Musts to avoid (7, 8)

Meaningless repetition

Not only must we avoid praying for the wrong reasons; we must also avoid 'babbling like pagans' (7a). Pagan worship was often characterised by the continuous repetition of incantations in an effort to elicit some form of response from the deities they were invoking. And it could go on for hours. The prophets of Baal are a good example of this, as they called on their god incessantly and more and more furiously for most of the day, much to the amusement of the prophet Elijah (1 Kings 18:26-29). We can also see similar characteristics in many other religions today.

Such a mechanical recitation of words is not prayer at all. Prayer is a personal and intimate communication between us and our loving heavenly Father, which stems from a sincere heart and a thoughtful mind, and is symptomatic of a growing and deepening relationship with God. Therefore, we need to be cautious about using certain aids to prayer, or prayers written by others, lest they lead us into mere repetition, rather than engaging both our hearts and our minds. This can happen just as much with extempore prayer, where the same form of words is used every time. Our prayers should be characterised by meaningful involvement, not meaningless detachment.

This is not to say that we must avoid repeating what we say to God in prayer. Persistence is an attribute which God expects to see in our praying, and this will obviously involve some repetition. Jesus Himself repeated His prayer in the Garden of Gethsemane (Matthew 26:44; Mark 14:39). The point Jesus is making is this: that whenever we pray, we must think through what we are saying; and that the words we utter must be a true expression of how we are feeling in our hearts.

Going on and on

But Jesus tells us that we must avoid going on and on when we pray, as the pagans do. We are not to be like them (8a). They mistakenly ' "think they will be heard because of their many words" ' (7b), when nothing could be further from the truth. It's not the words that count: it's the heart and the motive which matter. They are what God is interested in. He is not impressed by loquaciousness: though, judging by some of the prayers I've heard down the years, I find that this truth doesn't seem to have been grasped by some! D. L. Moody quipped: 'Some people's prayers need to be cut off at both ends and set on fire in the middle.' Augustine observed that 'We may pray most when we say least, and may pray least when we say most.'

And just to underline the point, Jesus then reminds us that ' "your Father knows what you need before you ask him" ' (8b). Which seems to make any words superfluous. 'So why bother praying at all?' we might reasonably ask. 'If God knows all our needs before we even speak a single word, why does He expect us to voice them to Him in prayer?' Simply because He wants us to invite Him into the situations of our own free will, thereby handing the problems over to Him completely to deal with in His way and in His time. This requires us to exercise our faith, thus demonstrating our trust in God. Laying our needs before Him is an expression of humility and an acknowledgement of our reliance upon God. All these are characteristics which God longs to see developing in us as we walk with Him.

On the subject of going on and on, I came across the following observation made by an American writer, in which he mentions 'The Lord's Prayer', the subject of the rest of this chapter. He was making the point that it's not how long we talk, it's what we say that is so important. This is what he wrote: 'The Lord's Prayer contains 52 words; the Gettysburg Address, 266; the Ten Commandments, 297; the Declaration of Independence, 300; and a recent U.S. government order setting the price of cabbage, 26,911.' I think that speaks for itself!

The Lord's Prayer (9-13)

Introduction

Having described the wrong way to pray, Jesus now outlines the right way by means of what has become known as 'The Lord's Prayer'. Some call it 'The Disciples' Prayer', thinking of those who would use it rather than of the Lord who gave it.

The Prayer is both a pattern for us to copy (9a), modelling our own prayers on it, and at the same time an actual prayer for us to use as it stands (Luke 11:2a). Considering it is recited countless times across the world every day, I find it perhaps surprising that rarely, in my experience, is a sermon preached specifically on its content.

The Prayer falls neatly into two sections, both of which contain three petitions. The first part focuses on God Himself. By contrast, the focus of the second part is our dependence upon Him.

Two truths

But before we get into the petitions, there is an opening phrase which sets the whole Prayer in context: 'Our Father in heaven' (9b). Jesus commands us to address God in this way to remind us of two truths which are vital to bear in mind whenever we come to pray.

The first is that we are entering the presence of a Person who loves us with an everlasting love, has redeemed us at great cost, and has brought us into His family. He is 'Our Father', with whom we have a special, intimate, personal relationship, and who has our best interests at heart. This is in complete contrast to portrayals of God in many other religions.

The second truth is that He is 'in heaven', reigning in awesome power, majesty and holiness; the great Creator of the world, the universe, and all that is in them. These great truths should cause praise and worship to well up within us, which in my experience is always the best way to begin a time of prayer.

Having been reminded of these truths, we shall now approach God in the right frame of mind, knowing that He will welcome us with love, that He will hear our petitions, and that He has the power to meet every need and to deal with every situation. This also helps us get our problems in perspective. Therefore, whenever we pray, we should come into His presence with confidence and boldness, yet at the same time with due deference and humility.

Name, kingdom and will

The first petition of this God-focused part of the Prayer is 'hallowed be your name' (9c). 'Hallowed' means 'treated as holy'. In biblical times, and still today in certain cultures of the world, the person's name is all important, because it actually stands for the person himself. So, when we say these words, we are in fact praying that God alone will be worshipped throughout the world, and that His holy name and that of His Son Jesus will be reverenced and lifted up in all nations of the earth, to the exclusion of all others, as it is in heaven.

The second petition is 'your kingdom come' (10a). Here we are praying that the Kingdom of God, which Jesus came to bring into the world, will continue to grow throughout all nations, as more and more people place Him on the throne of their hearts and submit to His kingly rule in their lives. We are also praying that Jesus will return very soon in power and glory, so that God's Kingdom may be fully established and all evil destroyed, as it is in heaven.

The third petition is 'your will be done on earth as it is in heaven' (10b). God's will is already being done in heaven, where everything is perfect as a result. We are praying that life here on earth may become more and more like that in heaven, and that God's purposes may be worked out in the world, as they are in heaven.

We can also apply these to our own lives by prayerfully asking ourselves these three questions each day. Firstly, 'Am I worshipping any other gods or owing allegiance to any other name?' Secondly, 'Is Jesus still on the throne of my heart, and am I living my life in submission to Him?' And thirdly, 'Am I being obedient to God's will so that His purposes can be worked out in my life?'

Physical, spiritual and moral

We now come to the second section of the Prayer. Having prayed that God may be glorified in all the earth, and by implication in our lives, we see that the focus of the Prayer switches to the needs and the well-being of the supplicants: physical, spiritual and moral.

• Bread

The first of the three petitions is 'Give us today our daily bread' (11). This is not an arrogant demand, as in 'You owe me, God!' Rather, it is a humble request which recognises that all our physical needs are daily supplied by the generous grace of God. It acknowledges our absolute and complete reliance on the provision of His hand for the necessities of our lives, which are essential for our physical well-being. It reminds us that we are totally dependent upon Him for the seeds to plant, and for the weather to cause them to grow into the wonderful variety of crops which abound on this amazing planet, whose hemispheres experience the seasons and harvest at different times of the year.

God has promised us that '"As long as the earth endures, seedtime and harvest, cold and heat, summer and winter, day and night will never cease"' (Genesis 8:22). We can therefore bring this petition before God with confidence, knowing that He has already pledged to fulfil it. How important it is that we do so each day, humbly confessing our daily dependence on God for the provision of our physical needs.

However, God doesn't put the bread on the table for us! We must plant, tend, harvest and distribute the crops ourselves. God provides; we divide: and, to our shame, our distribution is often not fairly done (Matthew 25:35a).

• Forgiveness

The second petition is 'Forgive us our debts, as we have also forgiven our debtors' (12). Luke's account renders this verse: 'Forgive us our sins, for we also forgive everyone who sins against us' (11:4a). The debt referred to in Matthew is clearly our sin, which deserves to be punished. But God in Jesus paid the price of that debt Himself on the cross, thus making it possible for our sins to be forgiven (Isaiah 53:5; Mark 10:45b; Acts 13:38; Romans 5:8; Ephesians 1:7). Again, we can bring this petition before God with confidence, because He has already promised us that 'If we confess our sins, he is faithful and just and will forgive us our sins and purify us from all unrighteousness' (1 John 1:9). How important it is that we do so each day, humbly confessing our daily need of God's forgiveness for our sinfulness.

However, unlike the other five petitions in the Prayer, this one comes with a condition attached. If we want God to forgive us, then we must forgive those who do wrong to us. This teaching is amplified in verses 14 and 15, which immediately follow the Prayer, and in the parable of the Unforgiving Servant, which Matthew records later in his gospel (18:23-35). Many issues are raised by this command to forgive. Extending forgiveness to others is absolutely essential for our spiritual well-being and progress.

It is important to understand that forgiving others doesn't mean that we can earn the right to God's forgiveness, but our very act of forgiveness shows three attributes on our part. Firstly, that each of us has a forgiving spirit, which is a major evidence of a person who is truly repentant for his own sins before God. Secondly, that we realise what we are asking God to do for us by doing it for others, and thus experiencing what is involved. Thirdly, that we have come to appreciate how small are the wrongs others have done to us, when set against the greatness of our sin against God. It was this very point that the master emphasised to the unforgiving servant in the parable (Matthew 18:32, 33). As Dr Martyn Lloyd-Jones wrote: 'I say to the glory of God and in utter humility that whenever I see myself before God and realise even something of what my blessed Lord has done for me, I am ready to forgive anybody anything.'

• Deliverance

The third petition consists of two that go together: 'And lead us not into temptation, but deliver us from the evil one' (13). The first part presents us with a problem, because it is inconceivable that God would deliberately lead us into temptation. As the epistle of James states: 'When tempted, no-one should say, "God is tempting me." For God cannot be tempted by evil, nor does he tempt anyone; but each one is tempted when, by his own evil desire, he is dragged away and enticed' (James 1:13, 14). Clearly, the enticer is 'the evil one', Satan himself. It is he who wants us to fall into temptation and revert to our old sinful ways, and we need God to deliver us from his wiles.

It is also the case that God allows us to be tested by means of all sorts of trials and temptations, so that we may develop as disciples, and emerge from such experiences stronger in our faith (James 1:2-4). So the question is, 'Why pray not to have to face them?' The most likely answer is that we are actually praying that we may overcome the trials and temptations, and not be overcome by them.

John Stott suggests a helpful paraphrase of the actual meaning of this petition: 'Do not allow us so to be led into temptation that it overwhelms us, but rescue us from the evil one.' Praise God that there is victory for us over all the devil's schemes in Christ Jesus! The apostle Paul encourages us with these words: 'Be strong in the Lord and in his mighty power. Put on the full armour of God so that you can take your stand against the devil's schemes' (Ephesians 6:10, 11).

We all have to face temptation, often on a daily basis. It comes in many forms, according to our own particular vulnerabilities. Sometimes it is so subtle that we don't even realise we are being sucked in. We need to be on our guard constantly. It is essential for our moral well-being that we recognise our reliance upon God to deliver us from the devil's machinations. How we need to pray daily that God will enable us to be victorious over these temptations, and to live lives that are upright before Him in this world!

At the same time, we must also do everything within our power to deal with any temptation that comes our way.

Sometimes we are our own worst enemies. As Robert Orbin remarked: 'Most people want to be delivered from temptation, but would like to keep in touch.' Erwin W. Lutzer wrote that 'Our response to temptation is an accurate barometer of our love for God.' What a challenging statement that is!

The apostle Paul also brings encouragement by reminding us that 'God is faithful; he will not let you be tempted beyond what you can bear. But when you are tempted, he will also provide a way out so that you can stand up under it' (1 Corinthians 10:13b). So we can bring this petition to God with confidence, knowing that He has promised to allow us to be tempted only to the extent that we can cope, and to bring us out of it triumphantly. How important it is that we do so each day, humbly confessing our daily dependence on God to deliver us from the evil one.

I cannot say

Someone once wrote: 'The entire Disciples' Prayer must be something that flows out of a truly committed heart. It ought to be a definition of your spirit, your attitude toward God, what is inside you.' Another author put it like this:

'I cannot say "our" if I live only for myself.

I cannot say "Father" if I do not endeavour each day to act like His child.

I cannot say "in heaven" if I am laying up no treasure there.

I cannot say "hallowed be Your name" if I am not striving for holiness.

I cannot say "Your kingdom come" if I am not doing all in my power to hasten that wonderful event.

I cannot say "Your will be done" if I am disobedient to His Word.

I cannot say "on earth as it is in heaven" if I'll not serve
    Him here and now.
I cannot say "Give us today our daily bread" if I am
    dishonest or seeking things by subterfuge.
I cannot say "Forgive us our debts" if I harbour a grudge
    against anyone.
I cannot say "Lead us not into temptation" if I deliberately
    place myself in its path.
I cannot say "Deliver us from evil" if I do not put on the
    whole armour of God.'

Whether we use this Prayer as a pattern for our own prayers, or recite it as it stands, may our lives be such that we are able do so with integrity.

Questions for group study

Matthew 6:1-18

Verses 1-6; 16-18

Background

1. What were the three prescribed religious duties?

Discuss

2. What challenge is Jesus bringing to His disciples here?

Apply

3. Why is this principle important for us?

Discuss

4. How were the Pharisees being hypocritical as they practised these religious obligations?
5. What did Jesus mean when He said that they 'have received their reward in full'?

Apply

6. How should we be different when we give, pray and fast?

Discuss

7. Why is secrecy important in these areas?
8. Why is fasting a neglected discipline in the lives of many Christians?

Apply

9. Should our church encourage fasting?

Discuss
10 In what ways does God reward us as we practise these disciplines for the right reasons?

Apply
11 What temptations does each of these disciplines present *not* to practise them for the right reasons?

Discuss
12 Is there a place for giving, prayer and fasting publicly?

Apply
13 What opportunities are there in our church for this?

Verses 7, 8

Discuss
14 What sort of repetition are we meant to avoid when praying?
15 What actually counts when we pray?

Apply
16 What dangers are there in using aids to prayer, or the same form of words each time we pray?
17 Are we persistent in our praying?

Discuss
18 What's the point in praying if God already knows what we need?

Verses 9-15

Discuss
19 What two aspects are there to 'The Lord's Prayer'?
20 What two sections does it fall into?
21 What two truths are vital to bear in mind whenever we come to pray?

Apply
22 How will bearing these truths in mind help us when we pray?

Discuss
23 When we say the following phrases, what are we praying will actually happen:
    'hallowed be your name';
    'your kingdom come';
    'your will be done on earth as it is in heaven' (11)?

Apply
24 What questions can we ask ourselves to see if we are applying these petitions to our own lives?

Discuss
25 Of what is the request for our daily bread a recognition, acknowledgement and reminder?

Apply
26 What confidence does Genesis 8:22 give us as we bring this petition?

Discuss
27 What is the debt referred to in verse 12?

Apply
28 What confidence does 1 John 1:9 give us as we bring this petition?

Discuss
29 What condition is attached to this petition?
30 What does the willingness to forgive show about the person forgiving?

Apply
31 To what extent can these attributes be seen in us?
32 Is the willingness to forgive one another a characteristic of our church?

Discuss
33 What are we actually praying in the third petition (13)?

Apply
34 What encouragement for this can we find in Ephesians 6:10, 11?

Discuss
35 What kinds of temptation do people face?
36 Do we agree that 'Our response to temptation is an accurate barometer of our love for God' [E. W. Lutzer]?

Apply

37 What confidence does 1 Corinthians 10:13b give us as we bring this petition?

For personal prayer and reflection

When I give money, pray, or fast, do I pass the secrecy test?
Is fasting something I should practise more than I do?
How would I respond to the sort of situation cited by Ruth Harms Calkin in her poem?
Are my prayers meaningless or meaningful?
Do my prayers demonstrate a faith and a trust in God?
Am I living my life in submission and obedience to God?
Am I willing to forgive those who have wronged me?
In what particular areas am I vulnerable to temptation?
Am I claiming victory through Christ in those areas?
Can I use 'The Lord's Prayer' with integrity?

CHAPTER 5

Dos and Don'ts

Matthew 6:19-7:6

Introduction
In each of the three sections contained within these verses, Jesus first of all tells His disciples not to do as the world does, and then follows it up by commanding them to do something completely different. Indeed, this is the main thrust of all the teaching contained within the Sermon on the Mount: that we, as disciples of Jesus Christ and members of the Kingdom of God, are expected to display characteristics and attitudes which are fundamentally different and distinct from those to be seen in the lives of people around us.

Desires (6:19-21, 24)

Heavenly or earthly?
The first of the three 'don'ts' is: '"Do not store up for your-

selves treasures on earth, where moth and rust destroy and thieves break in and steal"' (19). By contrast, we are told to do something very different: '"But store up for yourselves treasures in heaven, where moth and rust do not destroy, and where thieves do not break in and steal"' (20). And then Jesus explains the reason why this is so important for our lives: '"For where your treasure is, there your heart will be also"' (21). In other words, Jesus is asking each one of us, 'What is your heart set on? What do you treasure the most?' These questions probe the very depths of our being, and our answers reveal the desires of our hearts.

We live in a society where the hearts of most people are set on the things of this world alone. Their desires are plain to see: to accumulate as much money and as many possessions as possible, and to indulge themselves in experiencing as many pleasures as possible. But this is nothing new. Sinful mankind has always worshipped at the shrines of materialism and hedonism. For example, the excesses of the Roman Empire, which ruled Palestine at the time of Jesus, are well documented.

Jesus points out the foolishness of setting our hearts on, and placing our security in, such earthly things as these, which can come to an end at a moment's notice (19). In those days, there wasn't the comparative safety of banks, and robbery was commonplace. Indeed, everything His listeners possessed was subject to decay, corruption and theft. Even today, our money is susceptible to fraud, falls in the stock market, inflation, variations in the interest rate, not to mention being stolen in a robbery or a mugging.

Earthly treasure is never lasting, as opposed to heavenly treasure, which is everlasting. Therefore, as members of God's Kingdom, our aim should be to store up treasure in heaven. As the apostle Paul put it: 'Set your hearts on things above . . . not on earthly things' (Colossians 3:1, 2). God expects us to have heavenly desires, rather than earthly ones. And that may well call for a radical rethink on our part.

Storing up treasure

So how do we store up treasure in heaven? Although Jesus doesn't elaborate on this subject, it seems to me that we fulfil His command when we invest our lives in activities which yield eternal rather than temporal dividends, the value of which will be fully known only in heaven. Here are three suggestions of ways in which we may store up treasure in heaven, each of which reflects heavenly rather than earthly desires.

The first such area of activity could be described as evangelistic. This is where we seek to witness to others whenever the opportunities arise, stemming from a heavenly desire that they come to know Christ as their personal Lord and Saviour. Such witnessing takes many forms, including sharing our testimonies, getting alongside people and involving ourselves in their problems. Also, by being committed to the Church's outreach programmes, which communicate the Gospel to the local community in various appropriate ways, including social action programmes, which show the compassion of Christ to people; such actions often speak louder than any words.

Giving financially on a regular and sacrificial basis to the work of our church and any of the various Christian organisations that exist is another such activity; born of a heavenly desire to see the work of God's Kingdom progress. And it costs us to do it, in more ways than one! As Martin Luther astutely observed: 'There are three conversions necessary: the conversion of the heart, the mind and the purse. Of these three, it may well be that we moderns find the conversion of the purse the most difficult.'

The third area of activity takes place in our personal lives, as we seek to be obedient to God in all things, to submit ourselves to His will, to be faithful in prayer, to do good to others, to show the fruit of the Spirit, and to be salt and light for Him wherever He sends us. All these issuing from a heavenly desire to please God, to become more like Christ, and to be filled with His Holy Spirit. As we seek to do the work of the Kingdom of God, so we are storing up treasure in heaven.

Make your choice

However, in my opinion, it would be a mistake to conclude from these verses that Jesus is saying that having money or possessions is wrong, or that enjoying pleasurable experiences is undesirable. Not at all. It is only when our lives become dominated by them and revolve around them that we are guilty of succumbing to the lure of earthly desires.

We must not allow money, or anything else for that matter, to usurp God on the throne of our lives. As Jesus points out: '"No-one can serve two masters. Either he will hate the one and love the other, or he will be devoted to the one and despise the other. You cannot serve both God and Money"' (24).

The picture Jesus uses here is not about an employee working for two employers at the same time. Rather, it is an illustration taken from the practice of slavery, which was common throughout the Roman Empire at the time of Jesus, and is reflected in the writings of the apostle Paul. The slave was the property of his master, and could be bought and sold by him at will. He was part of the goods he owned. It was therefore impossible for the slave to belong to two masters simultaneously. Such a compromise could not exist.

Yet, in my experience, there are those who think they can serve both God and money, and see no reason to choose between the two. But this is to seek a compromise that cannot exist. If God does not receive our complete adoration and total devotion, then we are no longer serving Him properly with one hundred per cent commitment. We are therefore not serving Him at all, because He is no longer Lord; we are merely paying Him lip-service. Our earthly desires have prevailed, and money has become our god. We cannot escape the choice.

Love of money

The Pharisees were a prime example of people who thought they could do just that. Luke tells us: 'The Pharisees, who loved money, heard all this and were sneering at Jesus. He said to them, "You are the ones who justify yourselves in the eyes of men, but God knows your hearts. What is highly valued among men is detestable in God's sight"' (Luke 16:14, 15).

It's not money itself that is the problem: it is the *love* of money that is 'a root of all kinds of evil' (1 Timothy 6:10a). This was the problem the rich young ruler had, and Jesus knew it (Luke 18:18-27). So He said to him: '"Sell everything you have and give to the poor, and you will have treasure in heaven. Then come, follow me." When he heard this, he became very sad, because he was a man of great wealth' (18:22, 23). It was his love of money that was a barrier to his becoming a disciple of Jesus. His desire for earthly treasure had to be replaced with desire for heavenly treasure. He was hoping for a compromise, but he had to make a choice. I wonder how we would react if God told us to do something similar?

Trust (6:25-34)

Far more

The second 'don't' is 'do not worry'. But before these words comes the clause '"Therefore I tell you"' (25a). Jesus is linking what He is about to teach His disciples with what He has just been saying about choosing who our master will be.

And the connection is this: once we have decided to serve God, then it follows that this will have an impact on our priorities in life. No longer are we to make such matters as food and clothing our prime concerns, as the world so often does; there are far more important things in life for us. As Eugene H. Peterson renders it in The Message paraphrase: 'There is far more to your life than the food you put in your stomach, more to your outer appearance than the clothes you hang on your body' (25b). Jesus elaborates on this later (33).

Just look

This does not mean to say that food and clothing are unimportant: obviously, both are vital for our health and well-being. So much so, that God has provided the wherewithal in His wonderful creation for us to be able to meet these basic needs. So, no worries there then! Or there shouldn't be. Just look at the way your heavenly Father provides food for the birds, Jesus reminds us (26a). And as for clothes, Jesus continues, just look how beautifully arrayed the lilies of the field are (28). Not even King Solomon, a byword in his day for great splendour and magnificence, was in the same league as they (29).

The point being, that if God so provides food for the birds, and clothes the flowers with such beauty, even though they last but a moment (30), how much more will He provide for us?

'"Are you not much more valuable than they?"' asks Jesus, comparing us with the birds (26b). Not to be able to rest in God's promise of provision shows a lack of faith on our part (30b). We are to learn to trust God to provide for all our needs.

However, it would be a mistake to think this means that we are required to do nothing; that we just sit back and God will provide for us. The birds still have to forage for their food, even though '"your heavenly Father feeds them"' (26). Similarly, we have to work for our daily bread, although God has provided everything we need to ensure its supply. As the apostle Paul wrote: '"If a man will not work, he shall not eat"' (2 Thessalonians 3:10). This is not to deny that God does miraculously provide for His people at times of extremity; but this is the exception, not the rule.

In the rocking chair

In between the two examples He cites from nature, Jesus slips in a question which broadens the issue considerably: '"Who of you by worrying can add a single hour to his life?"' (27). This can also be translated: '"Who of you by worrying can add a single cubit [18 inches] to his height?"'

Before we go any further, it is important to understand that Jesus is addressing the kind of worry which gives rise to anxiety and has a negative effect on us, not that which evokes concern and stimulates us into action to solve the problem. Whichever rendering of the question we take, the meaning is clear: worrying about anything is a futile exercise, and shows a distinct lack of trust in God. As Oswald Chambers said: 'Worry is an indication that we think God cannot look after us.'

Bernard Meltzer commented thus on the futility of worry: 'Worry is like a rocking chair. It gives you something to do but doesn't get you anywhere.' Yet we all worry and get anxious about all sorts of things! It seems to be a part of the human condition. And from my own experience, I know how easy it is for worries to eat us up from the inside. There is a Jewish proverb which says: 'Worms eat you when you're dead; worries eat you when you're alive.' Someone once asked, 'Why let yourself be consumed by what's eating you?' King David, who experienced more troubles in his life than most of us ever will, had learnt the wisdom of trusting God in all situations, and brought his worries to Him in prayer: 'Search me, O God . . . and know my anxious thoughts' (Psalm 139:23).

An act of the will

How difficult it is at times to deal with the worries and anxieties that we experience. As Billy Graham remarked: 'When worry is present, trust cannot crowd its way in.' We have to make it an act of the will to trust God. David had to exercise such will-power many times, as we see in his psalms. Perhaps the best example of this is to be found in Psalm 56, which he wrote when he lived among the Philistines to escape from Saul; a very anxious time for him indeed (1 Samuel 21:10-15). In that psalm, we can imagine David's battle within himself as he says to God: 'When I am afraid, I will trust in you. In God, whose word I praise, in God I trust; I will not be afraid' (Psalm 56:3, 4). He repeats this act of will to trust God later in the psalm, which emphasises what a struggle he found it.

I find this very encouraging and instructive. Encouraging, because if a man like David, who was so close to God, was at times overwhelmed by anxious thoughts and worries, then it's not surprising that the rest of us experience similar difficulties. Instructive, because it shows us how to respond at those times:

to bring our anxieties to God in prayer, and to trust Him no matter what. As someone once said: 'Why worry when you can pray?' Prayer is an acknowledgement of our faith and trust in God; worry is a denial that such faith and trust exist. Worry and trust are mutually exclusive. Another author wrote: 'When we worry, we believe more in our problems than in God's promises.'

Run after

Having reminded His hearers of God's loving concern for their physical welfare by means of examples taken from nature (26, 28-30), Jesus now returns to the matter of what we should make the priorities in our lives, having owned Him as our Master.

A good way of seeing the priorities of any society is to browse along the magazine section of a large newsagent's. Many of the contents are to do with food and clothing. There seems to be a food-and-fashion culture abroad in society, with a proliferation of such magazines, and also television programmes, presenting us with foods and clothes from all over the world. We are continually encouraged to experiment with all sorts of weird and wonderful recipes by a variety of celebrity cooks, and to wear the latest fashions: if we can still get in them after eating all that food!

There is no doubt that many people still 'run after all these things', just as the pagans of old did (32a). Now, there is nothing wrong in enjoying different foods and wearing good clothes, if you can afford them, of course! But Jesus reminds us that '"your heavenly Father knows that you need them"' (32b), so such matters are no longer to be our priority. Rather, what we are to do is to '"seek first his kingdom and his righteousness"', with the promise that '"all these things will be given to you as well"' (33). Jesus is saying that the spiritual dimension to our lives is far more important than the physical. The world we live in has these priorities back to front; indeed, the spiritual is apparently non-existent in the lives of many, which makes them no different in essence from the pagans Jesus referred to.

By telling us to 'seek first his kingdom and his righteousness', Jesus is commanding us to make the work of God's Kingdom and doing what is right in God's sight our priorities. It is these that we should 'run after'; and He expects to see evidence of them in our daily living. In practical terms, this means that our lives are to be characterised by a willingness to do the following: serve God alone and do His will; obey and trust Him in all things; live in a holy and upright way; share our faith with others; show the compassion of Christ to people; give our time, effort, resources and money to the work of the Kingdom as outworked in the local church; engage with the social problems around us, and work for justice in the world. And the promise is that, as we make these our priorities, everything else will fall into place. The challenging question we all have to answer is: What am I running after?

Safer than a known way

This whole section of teaching began with 'Therefore' (25), and the end of it is prefaced by the same word: '"Therefore do not worry about tomorrow, for tomorrow will worry about itself. Each day has enough trouble of its own"' (34). Thus Jesus is linking this verse with everything that has gone before.

Jesus is saying that once we have learnt to trust God, and have sorted our priorities, there is no need to be consumed with fearful worry about what the future holds any more. The rocking chair can be disposed of. We can rest in God, entrusting tomorrow to Him, knowing that everything is in His hands, that nothing takes Him by surprise, and that He will be there to help us to deal with whatever may occur when the time comes. As the songwriter put it: 'I know not what the future holds, but I know who holds the future.' Ralph Waldo Emerson expressed it this way: 'All I have seen teaches me to trust the Creator for all I have not seen.'

Planning for tomorrow and worrying about tomorrow are two very different things. The former shows a responsible attitude; the latter indicates a lack of trust in God. Jesus is telling us to live a day at a time. '"One day's trouble is enough for one day"' (34b) is how J. B. Phillips translates the final sentence. If we bring worries about tomorrow into today, we shall experience overload. Someone put it like this: 'Your ship is equal to the load of today; but when you are carrying yesterday's worry and tomorrow's anxiety, lighten up or you will sink.'

On 3 September 1939, Britain declared war on Nazi Germany, and the future looked very bleak indeed. As part of his Christmas message in that year of acute anxiety and intense uncertainty, King George VI quoted from the author M. Louise Haskins some words which speak about the wisdom of trusting in God, whatever the situation: 'I said to the man who stood at the gate of the year, "Give me a light, that I may tread safely into the unknown." And he replied, "Go out into the darkness, and put your hand into the hand of God. That shall be to you better than light, and safer than a known way."'

Judgements (7:1-6)

There are times

The third 'don't' is 'Do not judge' (7:1a). At first sight, it would seem that Jesus is forbidding us ever to make any kind of judgement or form opinions which are critical of anyone. But that would mean Jesus is actually encouraging us to turn a blind eye to wrongdoing, which is certainly not in accord with the rest of His teachings.

For example, later in this chapter He instructs us to expose false teachers (15-20), a command reflected elsewhere in the New Testament (2 Corinthians 11:12-15; 1 John 4:1-3). On another occasion, Jesus also set out the steps to be taken by an individual, supported by the church, in the case of a brother who 'sins against you' (Matthew 18:15-17). The subject of the church's disciplining its membership and judging their actions features in the letter of the apostle Paul to the church in Corinth, in which he instructs them to expel the immoral brother (1 Corinthians 5:1, 2, 12, 13).

So there are times when judgements have to be made, and it is at such times that we need to seek God's wisdom and discernment, so that the correct decisions may be made, and the correct actions taken.

He alone

So what does Jesus mean when He says that we are not to judge? He is commanding us not to display a judgemental, faultfinding, critical attitude towards others, the sole purpose of which is to tear people down. Setting ourselves up in judgement over other people in this way betrays a superior and arrogant self-righteousness, which has no place in the heart of a member of God's Kingdom.

Yet how often are we guilty of precisely this: of acting as judge, jury and executioner on another person? And often towards a fellow-Christian at that! And this rash sentence is usually passed without our knowing the circumstances, let alone caring about the full facts. There is a Native American proverb which says: 'Don't judge any man until you have walked two moons in his moccasins.' The German author Goethe put it like this: 'Don't judge anyone harshly until you yourself have been through his experiences.'

But it is so tempting to judge others: to evaluate their behaviour, their attitudes, even their commitment to Christ; especially so if we want to compare ourselves favourably with them. The inevitable result of this is that ill-conceived and usually false conclusions are drawn. Only God knows the person's heart, and only God knows the full facts of the situation, so only God can judge with justice and fairness. Therefore we are to leave any judging that needs to be done to the One who is all-seeing and all-knowing. As Oswald Chambers said: 'The Holy Ghost alone is in the true position of a critic.' He continued with these significant words: 'He is able to show what is wrong without wounding or hurting.'

And in any case, we are in no position to judge anyone else, being sinners ourselves! As William Shakespeare succinctly put it: 'Forebear to judge, for we are sinners all.' We are just as bad as those whom we are presuming to condemn. The apostle Paul wrote: 'You, therefore, have no excuse, you who pass judgement on someone else, for at whatever point you judge the other, you are condemning yourself, because you who pass judgement do the same things' (Romans 2:1). Only God is holy and without sin. Therefore, it is He alone who has the right to judge.

Measure for measure
Jesus goes on to warn us that if we do have the temerity to judge

others, then '"you too will be judged. For in the same way you judge others, you will be judged"' (1b, 2a). It seems to me that this can be applied to us in two ways. Firstly, that if we judge others, we in turn will find ourselves being judged by people in the same way and to the same extent that we have judged them. Which raises the pertinent question: How would I like to be judged solely on the perceptions people have of me and my situation, on hearsay and gossip, rather than on the truth of the matter? Secondly, that when we judge others we place ourselves under God's judgement. We are accountable to Him for our arrogant and critical attitude. We will be judged for presuming to judge in God's place.

Jesus goes on to say: '"and with the same measure you use, it will be measured to you"' (2b). Luke gives a fuller account of Jesus' words at this point: '"Forgive, and you will be forgiven. Give, and it will be given to you. A good measure, pressed down, shaken together and running over will be poured into your lap"' (Luke 6:37, 38). In other words, *don't* be judgemental and critical; *do* be forgiving, generous and compassionate instead. This is what God expects to see in our lives. And, in matters such as these, God's attitude to us is determined by our attitude to others. If we forgive others their sins against us, then He will forgive us all our sins against Him, which are far more. If we give generously to others, He will pour an abundance of blessings upon us which we shall hardly be able to contain.

Paul Tournier observed the amazingly beneficial effects on people's development when they were loved and encouraged rather than judged and criticised. He wrote: 'By seeing the tremendous blossoming which a person can experience when surrounded by love and confidence, when he does not feel judged, we can measure the stifling power of other people's criticism.'

I see no plank!

As we have seen elsewhere, there are occasions when Jesus uses dramatic pictures to explain His teachings; and here we find another example of this (3-5). I imagine that this illustration came straight out of His own personal experiences while working for many years in His father's carpentry workshop in Nazareth with His brothers James, Joseph, Simon and Judas (Matthew 13:55). I wonder how many times Jesus had taken a speck of sawdust out of their eyes, or even had one taken out of His own by them? The most likely time when specks of sawdust would have been flying around was while they were sawing up planks of wood to the required lengths. Interestingly, both a speck and a plank feature prominently in this illustration.

• Perception

There are two aspects to this scenario. The first concerns our perception (3). How ridiculous it is that we can clearly see the speck of sawdust in our brother's eye, while at the same time being totally oblivious to this great big plank of wood sticking out of our own eye! Jesus asks us why we are looking judgementally at the speck and ignoring the plank. By implication Jesus is saying that our perception is all wrong. We should be far more concerned about the plank in our own eye than the speck in our brother's. Why are we not dealing with our own major and rather obvious problems, rather than fixing our critical sights on the minor fault in our brother's life? Why is our focus on his shortcomings, and not on our own?

It is so much easier to judge others than to judge ourselves;

to see the faults of others rather than our own; to point out what is wrong in the lives of others rather than to deal with what is wrong in our own. 'Plank? What plank?' we ask. Jesus requires us to refocus our perception so we see the plank rather than the speck.

• Proposal

The second aspect concerns our proposal (4). Unbelievably, we are now proposing to help our brother by removing the speck in his eye, while still having this plank in our own! This is not only ludicrous; it is also dangerous. It could cause our brother great harm were we to pursue it. We may now be aware of the plank of our own faults, but we still haven't done anything about it. It's just as if we're pretending it's not actually there, while we continue to be judgemental towards our brother.

And therein lies our hypocrisy: pretending to have no faults when we have as many as anyone else; pretending to be right in the sight of God when we're not. There is a further pretence here. This supposedly kindly act of removing the speck from our brother's eye springs from a wrong motive. We are hypocritically pretending to do it for the good of our brother; but the fact that we have not yet dealt with the plank shows that we are acting out of a desire to enhance our own reputation, rather than out of compassion. This makes us no better than those hypocrites, the Pharisees, whose whole lives were a pretence, and whose motives Jesus had already fiercely exposed.

'First'

Jesus doesn't mince His words. '"You hypocrite,"' He says to us, '"first take the plank out of your own eye, and then you will see clearly to remove the speck from your brother's eye"' (5).

In other words, *don't* judge others, but *do* judge yourself; and then take the appropriate action to deal with the faults and shortcomings identified through this self-examination. Significantly, Jesus expects us to do this 'first', before doing anything else.

There are two other points to notice here. Firstly, that God doesn't remove the 'plank' from our eye: we do. Not only do we have to see it there; we have to decide to take it out of our eye. Of course, God will strengthen us and help us to do this as we call on Him in prayer. But we have to take the initiative in removing the 'plank', and purpose not to allow those failings or that wrongdoing to occur in our lives again.

Secondly, that wrongdoing by others is not to be ignored: the 'speck' is to be removed from our brother's eye. But we must be aware of our own 'planks' whenever we feel critical of others, and deal with them 'first' before God. Then we will be in a position to be able to help our brother with the fault that is plaguing him. There will no longer be a critical spirit or a judgemental attitude about us, but rather a genuine desire to help a fellow brother or sister in Christ to deal with his or her problems. Now our aim is to build people up, not to tear them down.

Someone once said: 'The person who has a true Christian spirit never takes delight in the faults of others.' Alice Duer Miller endorsed this when she gave this helpful guidance: 'If it's very painful for you to criticise your friends, you're safe in doing it. But if you take the slightest pleasure in it, that's the time to hold your tongue.'

Casting stones
The French author Honoré de Balzac once commented: 'The

more one judges, the less one loves.' We need to be constantly on guard against a critical spirit and a judgemental attitude such as the Pharisees had. To help us to do this, we need to ask ourselves regularly such questions as: Am I building people up or tearing them down? Do I encourage people or demolish them? Do I see people's virtues or only their faults? Do I apply the same zealous censure to myself that I do to others? As the apostle Paul wrote, presumably with these verses in mind: 'But if we judged ourselves, we would not come under judgement' (1 Corinthians 11:31).

Marilyn Morgan Helleberg tells the story of an incident which happened at a church camp she attended when a teenager. She recounts how 'An ugly rumour about two of the counsellors quickly became the talk of the camp. The next day, at morning prayer, the minister read the story of the adulterous woman, in which Jesus told the crowd that any person who had no sin could cast the first stone (John 8:1-11). And one by one, those who had come to stone her to death walked away. Then the minister passed around a bucket of stones and insisted that we each take one and carry it in our pocket throughout the remainder of camp. Any time we felt like criticising someone else, or talking behind another's back or passing on an ugly rumour, we were to reach into the pocket, touch the stone and ask ourselves if we were without sin.'

Marilyn goes on to say, and to pray: 'It's so easy to criticise others; only God knows a person's heart. Lord, prevent me from casting stones.' May that be our prayer, too.

Pigs, pearls and pointlessness

At the end of this section, there is another *don't* to be found which seems to stand on its own. At first sight, it might appear to have nothing to do with what has gone before. But on closer examination we can clearly see that it does actually involve making judgements about people, and being discerning in how we share spiritual truth with them. God expects us to make such judgements, not out of arrogance or criticism, but out of a deep concern that the message of the Kingdom be communicated appropriately.

There are actually two *don'ts* here which go together: '"Do not give dogs what is sacred; do not throw your pearls to pigs."' Jesus then continues: '"If you do, they may trample them under their feet, and then turn and tear you to pieces"' (6). 'What is sacred' and 'pearls' (see also Matthew 13:45, 46), are terms which Jesus uses to represent the message of the Kingdom and the good news which He came to bring.

• Not just yet

It seems to me that there are three possible interpretations of these words. The first one is applicable specifically to the period of Jesus' earthly ministry. At that time, the Gentiles were commonly and contemptuously referred to as 'dogs' by the Jews (see Matthew 15:26, 27). 'Pigs' also had a Gentile connection, as no Jew would keep them. They were unclean animals according to the Law of Moses (Leviticus 11:2-8; Deuteronomy 14:8).

Jesus was saying that the message which He brought was for the Jews. God had been preparing them for His coming and for the message that He would bring for thousands of years. The Gentiles, who had not been so prepared, would therefore not understand it. Consequently, they would treat it with contempt, and might even turn nasty about it. Therefore, it was pointless to go to the Gentiles with the good news of Jesus at that moment. The time would come later, and did so at the Ascension, when Jesus gave His disciples what has become known as 'The Great Commission' (Matthew 28:18-20).

• Shake the dust
The second interpretation casts in the role of the 'dogs' and the 'pigs' those who, in the words of John Calvin, 'by clear evidences, have manifested a hardened contempt of God, so that their disease appears to be incurable.' It is pointless to keep on sharing the Gospel with those who are so antagonistically opposed to its message. This doesn't mean to say that we should ever give up on such people: just that our time is better spent with those who do show some interest in the Gospel.

This principle can be seen in Jesus' instruction to the disciples as He sends them out with the message of the Kingdom (Matthew 10:14), and in the ministry of the apostle Paul as he preaches the Gospel (Acts 13:51; 18:5, 6). On each occasion, it is a matter of shaking the dust from off their feet when they are rejected, and moving on to pastures new, where there may be a receptiveness to the message.

• Consider the capacity
The third interpretation is that we need to be wise in our teaching of God's word. We are all at different stages of maturity in our relationship with God, and this will inevitably affect our capacity for understanding spiritual truths. For example, it is pointless and unfair to plunge a new Christian into the depths of the doctrinal 'deep end' when what he really needs is to learn to swim in the 'shallow end' of the basics of the faith. This is not to say that these basic truths are shallow: just that this is where he needs to start so that he may progress smoothly and

successfully into deeper waters of understanding in time.

It is vital that these considerations are borne in mind when we plan the teaching programmes in our churches. If not, we run the risk of having a church full of confused Christians, who do not fully appreciate or understand the pearls which are to be found in the sacred treasure chest of Scripture.

Questions for group study

Matthew 6:19-7:6

Chapter 6, verses 19-21, 24

Discuss
1. What sort of things are the hearts of most people in our society set on?
2. Why are such desires foolish?

Apply
3. What should our hearts be set on?

Discuss
4. How do we store up treasure in heaven?

Apply
5. What implications does this have for us in these areas:
   Our witnessing;
   Our financial giving;
   Our personal lives?

Background
6. Why was it impossible for a slave in Roman times to serve two masters?

Discuss
7. What teaching does Jesus give by means of this illustration?

Apply

8 With this in mind, what do we need to make sure is not happening in our lives?

Discuss

9 Why was selling everything he possessed the only way the rich young ruler could 'have treasure in heaven' (Luke 18:22)?

Apply

10 What can we learn from this about discipleship?

11 How would we react if Jesus told us to do the same?

Verses 25-34

Discuss

12 What connection does Jesus make between choosing whom our master will be, and matters like food and clothing?

13 Why does Jesus talk about the birds and the lilies of the field (26, 28-30)?

Apply

14 What confidence does this give us?

Discuss

15 What kind of worrying is Jesus talking about in verse 27?

16 Why is it difficult not to be eaten up with worry from time to time?

Apply

17 What sort of situations are most likely to cause us to experience such negative anxiety?

18 How should we deal with such worry?

19 What encouragement and help can we find in the experience of King David? (See Psalm 56).

Discuss

20 How are many people today similar to the 'pagans' of old?

21 What does Jesus say should be our priorities?

Apply

22 How can we show these priorities in our lives?

Discuss

23 What is the difference between *planning* for tomorrow and *worrying about* tomorrow?

Chapter 7, verses 1, 2

Background

24 In what situations does the Bible tell us that God actually expects us to judge others?

Discuss

25 What does Jesus mean when He says we are not to judge?

Apply
26 Why is it tempting to judge others in the very ways we are commanded not to?

Discuss
27 Why are we to leave judgement to God alone?

Apply
28 Why are we in no position to judge others anyway?
29 What will happen to us if we do judge others? (See verses 1b, 2).
30 What can we learn from Luke 6:37, 38 about the attitude God expects to see us adopting?

Verses 3-6
Discuss
31 What is Jesus saying is wrong about our perception?

Apply
32 Why is it much easier to judge others than to judge ourselves?

Discuss
33 What is wrong with our proposal to take the speck out of our brother's eye?
34 Why is such an act hypocritical?

Apply

35 Why do we, rather than God, have to take the initiative in removing the plank?

36 Why is it that only then are we truly able to help our brother with his problems?

37 What sort of questions do we need to ask ourselves, in order to guard against developing a critical spirit and a judgemental attitude?

38 Do we need to repent of casting stones at others in our church?

Discuss

39 How does verse 6 link in with the previous verses in this section?

40 What do the terms *'what is sacred'* and *'pearls'* represent?

41 If the *'dogs'* and *'pigs'* represent the Gentiles, what point is Jesus making here?

42 What other groups of people might they represent?

Apply

43 In this latter case, what implications does that have for us?

Discuss

44 What other interpretation of these words is possible?

Apply

45 What implications would such an understanding have for the teaching programmes in our churches?

For personal prayer and reflection

Are my desires earthly or heavenly?
In what ways am I storing up treasure in heaven?
Is Jesus truly the Lord of my life?
About what particular anxiety do I need to put my trust in God?
What impact is serving God having on my priorities?
Are they different from those of the world?
Am I guilty of being judgemental towards others?
Am I prepared to be forgiving, generous and compassionate instead?
Is there a plank that I need to remove?
Do I build people up or tear them down?
Which of the three 'Don'ts' causes me the most problems, and why?

CHAPTER **6**

Four Twos

Matthew 7:7-29

Two sides (7-11)

Jesus now returns to the subject of prayer. In Luke's account, these verses come immediately after Jesus has told the parable of the Friend at Midnight (Luke 11:5-10), which teaches that God expects us to be persistent in our prayers. Jesus emphasises this teaching here by making the same point in three different ways (7-8).

Triple emphasis

• Ask
We are to ask, and it will be given to us. Any child who really wants something doesn't just ask for it once: he keeps on and on about it, just to make sure his parents get the message. Our Father God wants us, His children, to ask like that.

I must have been a real pain one year in the months leading up to Christmas. There was a particular toy I had set my heart on, and from September onwards I kept on talking about this particular thing day after day. And every time we went shopping, I would drag my parents past the shop and point it out to them, just so they could be in no doubt about what I wanted for Christmas. I'm pleased to say that my persistence paid off, and on Christmas Day there it was.

• Seek

We are to seek, and we shall find what we are looking for. Seeking involves whole-hearted commitment: it takes time, effort and a single-minded determination. When I was a child, we used to play 'Hide and Seek', sometimes round the stooks in the cornfield. Hiding was easy; seeking was hard work. It was tiring, time-consuming and frustrating, particularly when you had relatives like mine, who would sneak from one stook to another when I wasn't looking. No wonder I couldn't find them!

The challenge to us is to be like the people in the time of King Asa, of whom it is said that 'They entered into a covenant to seek the Lord, the God of their fathers, with all their heart and soul' (2 Chronicles 15:12).

• Knock

We are to knock, and the door will be opened to us. If we go to visit someone, and he does not respond to our first knock on the door, it would be unusual if we were to leave the matter there. We are far more likely to keep on knocking until there is a response. I am sure there are times when we miss out on God's blessings because we stop knocking too soon.

Celestial vending machine

The use of the word 'will' (7) is so encouraging, because it means that a response is guaranteed. When we ask, God will answer; request and response are the two sides to prayer. However, that answer may be different from the one we are hoping for; and it may even be 'No', or 'Wait'. We considered various reasons elsewhere why answers to prayer do not often come immediately, so I shall not reiterate them here.

However, there is another important issue that we need to address. Some people have mistakenly thought these verses mean that God will grant us anything we ask for. But that would be to assume that God is at our beck and call, and is nothing more than a celestial vending machine: we slot in the prayer, and out pops the answer! It is important to understand that we must be praying in accordance with the teachings of Scripture, and subject to the sovereign will of God. For example, prayers for more love, strength, wisdom, discernment and understanding will be answered, whereas prayers for one million pounds for our own personal use are likely to go unheeded!

How much more

Jesus goes on to draw a comparison between the response of an earthly father and our heavenly Father to a request made by His child (9-11). Again, Jesus uses dramatic imagery to make His point. No good earthly father would dream of responding to requests for bread and fish by giving his child stones and snakes instead. It is unthinkable. He would give only that which was good, helpful, wholesome and beneficial to his child.

If earthly parents, who are capable of doing evil and wicked things, can find it in their hearts to respond lovingly to the requests of their children, continues Jesus, then 'how much more' will your heavenly Father, who is holy and perfect in all His ways, respond to your prayers out of a heart filled with divine love: a love that only wants what is best for you, and knows what is good for you. In other words, if you can do it, God certainly can, and will, and better, and abundantly!

How wonderful to know that when we come to God in prayer we are approaching a heavenly Father who loves us and is just waiting to shower His blessings upon us. Yet how often we fall short in prayer. God expects it to be a characteristic of our relationship with Him, and longs to hear from us. The parents among us would consider it a cause for concern if we never received any requests from our children. We would wonder what had gone wrong and whether they still loved and trusted us. Perhaps we can use these thoughts to reflect on the current state of our relationship with our heavenly Father.

Two Roads (13-14)

Leicester or Wisbech?

When I was a schoolteacher, I used to walk to and from work along a busy road which served our housing estate. I was often stopped by motorists and asked for directions. One day I was stopped by such a driver; and to this day I find it difficult to believe the conversation which ensued.

The motorist lowered the window, leant across, and asked me how to get to the A47. When I told her she was going in the wrong direction at the moment, her reply was, 'I haven't got to turn the car *round*, have I?' Not knowing quite how to respond, I soldiered on by telling her to turn left at the first roundabout, then left at the second, and so on. To this she replied, 'I don't like all these roundabouts!', in a tone which indicated that she held me personally responsible for each and every one of them. Remembering just in time that long-suffering is a fruit of the Spirit, which should be evident in my life, I ventured the helpful piece of information that when she saw the hospital on her left, she would be almost at the A47. To this she replied, 'I've already been past that hospital once!' I gritted my teeth, and politely asked whether she wanted to go in the direction of Leicester or Wisbech when she reached the junction of the A47. 'Leicester or Wisbech?' she echoed: 'I just want the A47!'

A choice to be made

Whether she liked it or not, that lady motorist was going to have to make a choice when she finally arrived at that junction – which I presume she eventually did! In these verses, Jesus sets out before us a far more important choice of roads: a choice which will have far-reaching consequences for us, both in this life and the next; a choice that will determine the direction of our lives, and our eternal destination. There is no 'third way'; we have to make a choice.

There are only two possible ways for us to go. Either we choose the 'broad' road, which we enter by means of the 'wide' gate; or we decide to walk the 'narrow' road, which is accessed through the 'small' and 'narrow' gate. Jesus urges us to choose the 'narrow' road because it 'leads to life', rather than the 'broad' road which 'leads to destruction'. He doesn't want any of us to choose the way whose ultimate end is destruction, because He is 'not wanting anyone to perish' (2 Peter 3:9). So much so, that Jesus has come to earth specifically to make it possible for each one of us to enjoy eternal life in heaven with Him for ever. In one of the best-known verses in the whole of

Scripture, Jesus says: ' "For God so loved the world that he gave his one and only Son, that whoever believes in him *shall not perish, but have eternal life"* ' (John 3:16; emphasis mine). God loves us so much that He wants us to choose the way that 'leads to life'; and that love cost Him His life. Having chosen the 'narrow' road, Jesus expects us to live our lives according to His teachings, which will guide us lovingly along the way that 'leads to life'.

The gate and the way
The gate to the narrow road is described as 'narrow'. This is not because it is difficult to get through, but because the gate is actually a Person, and one Person alone. As Jesus said on another occasion: ' "I am the gate; whoever enters through me will be saved" ' (John 10:9a). In another uncompromising statement, Jesus said of Himself: ' "I am the way and the truth and the life. No-one comes to the Father except through me" ' (John 14:6).

We live in a world of many faiths and beliefs, where tolerance, inclusiveness, equality and diversity are the buzz words. We want to be able to make our own choices, and not be told that there is a right way and a wrong way. 'All roads lead to God' is a popular maxim. Not according to Jesus they don't: and He should know, because He *is* God! Jesus made it quite clear that there is only one road which ends in heaven, and that is the way entered only through Him. All other roads are but one: the way of error, the wrong way. That is why it is described as 'broad': because it encompasses all other so-called 'ways'.

And the gate to it is 'wide', so it's easy to get on to. No repentance required at this gate: just stroll on through, bringing whatever ideas, moral values and attitudes you like. No one will tell you what to do on this road; you can please yourself and do exactly what you want; all creeds are welcome here. Not like being on that 'narrow' road, where there are clearly defined parameters and expectations, which take some living up to.

Such perceived restrictions are unpopular today, as people want to make up their own rules as they go along, frequently ending up in a complete mess, and living lives with no real purpose or meaning. They prefer this to living by a God-given framework which covers all eventualities, and enables them to live truly fulfilled lives which have both purpose and meaning. However, walking God's way doesn't mean we will never mess things up or wander off the road. But it does mean that God is right there with us to help us deal with our problems, and lovingly to guide us back on to the right way once again.

The statement that 'only a few find it' was particularly applicable to the beginnings of Christianity rather than now, when it has the largest number of adherents world-wide of any religion. However, it is still a poignant remark for many of us who live in countries where we seem to be very much in the minority. As we continue to walk God's way, let's do so in a manner which is attractive to people on the other road. May they see something different and appealing in our lifestyle which will challenge them to re-evaluate their own, to think about their eternal destination, and to respond to the claims of Jesus as the only gate and the only way to God.

Two Tests (15-23)

The fruit test (15-20)

Wolf warning
Jesus knew that, down through the years, the church would be

infiltrated by many false prophets, who would bring teachings which were a subtle blend of truth and error, and would lead many Christians astray. On this and on other occasions, He warned His disciples to be constantly on the look-out for such people (Matthew 24:11, 24; Mark 13:22). False prophets were certainly active in the early church. The apostle Paul encountered them (Acts 13:6), and wrote about them (2 Corinthians 11:13). In his first epistle, John strongly advised his readers to 'test the spirits to see whether they are from God, because many false prophets have gone out into the world' (1 John 4:1).

But it is Peter who really goes to town on this subject: it is the reason why he writes his second letter. He is forthright in his warnings about false teachers, scathing about their characteristics, and uncompromising about their fate. Having reminded his readers that false prophets were active in the time of the Old Testament prophets, he goes on to warn them that such people will appear in the church, leading many astray: 'But there were also false prophets among the people, just as there will be false teachers among you. They will secretly introduce destructive heresies, even denying the sovereign Lord who bought them – bringing swift destruction on themselves. Many will follow their shameful ways and will bring the way of truth into disrepute. In their greed these teachers will exploit you with stories they have made up' (2 Peter 2:1-3a).

Wolf wear

Part of the subtlety of the strategy of the false prophets is that the purpose of their arrival in the church is not immediately obvious. Having warned us to be on the look-out for them, Jesus then warns us that we won't recognise them for what they actually are, to begin with: ' "Watch out for false prophets.

They come to you in sheep's clothing, but inwardly they are ferocious wolves" ' (15).

These 'wolves' appear to be as innocent and harmless as sheep in a field. They ingratiate themselves with everyone, and are welcomed as part of the flock of God. They may be ordinary members of the church, but they may equally be ministers, leaders, or renowned speakers. Once accepted and trusted in this way, they begin to develop their hidden agendas. These are to devour as many of the flock as possible by means of their teaching, which is always a subtle blend of truth and error, and to scatter the rest of the sheep in confusion. The result of this infiltration is at best a divided church, and at worst a church completely torn apart and destroyed. Either way, the Christian witness of that church is derided, and Satan rejoices.

The apostle Paul was very concerned about this happening in the church at Ephesus, and he spoke prophetically to the elders of the church there: 'Keep watch over yourselves and all the flock of which the Holy Spirit had made you overseers. Be shepherds of the church of God. . . . I know that after I leave, savage wolves will come in among you and will not spare the flock. Even from your own number men will arise and distort the truth in order to draw away disciples after them. So be on your guard! Remember that for three years I never stopped warning each of you night and day with tears' (Acts 20:28-31).

In spite of Jesus' warning not to be deceived by outward appearances, too many of us still are. The history of the church is littered with such examples, which have resulted in many Christians being led astray and the Gospel being ridiculed. The deceptions still continue to this day, and will do so until Jesus comes again. How we need to be on our guard, and to test everything we hear against what the

Bible says, irrespective of where the words are coming from!

Wolf wise

Jesus tells us we can identify such people by applying a particular test: ' "By their fruit you will recognise them" ' (16a). He then goes on to explain that just as trees and plants bear fruit only of their own kind, and bad trees never produce good fruit, so we can pick out false prophets by looking at their fruit (16b-18, 20). And when such persons are identified, God expects us to deal drastically with them (19). They are not to be tolerated; they are to be removed permanently. The Ephesian elders took heed of Paul's warning. They applied the fruit test, and rejected the teaching of the Nicolaitans (Revelation 2:2b, 6), unlike the church at Pergamum, who accommodated them, and were rebuked for so doing (2:14-16). The church at Thyatira were also admonished for tolerating the teachings of 'that woman Jezebel, who calls herself a prophetess' (2:20a).

There are two particular areas where this fruit test needs to be rigorously applied. Firstly, we need to examine closely the fruit of their lives: their characteristics, conduct, attitudes and actions. We should ask ourselves whether they are living in accordance with the demands of God's Word, and if the fruit of the Spirit (Galatians 5:22, 23) are evident in their lives.

Secondly, we need to pay close attention to the fruit of their mouths (Luke 6:45): to analyse exactly what they are teaching, and the effect that this is having on the church. Is what they are saying doctrinally sound, particularly with regard to the person of Christ? John was very strong about this in his epistles (1 John 2:22; 2 John:7-9). Is this teaching building people up in their faith, or causing them to stumble? The apostle Paul was certainly concerned about this matter (2 Timothy 2:16-18). Is this teaching edifying the church, or causing divisions? Paul instructed Titus to take decisive action on this issue in the Cretan church (Titus 1:9-11).

Unfortunately, some Christians still seem to prefer to base their judgement on other factors rather than applying the fruit test, and consequently they are deceived by honeyed words, a handsome appearance, an appealing style, or a charismatic personality. May God give each one of us, and especially our church leaders, the wisdom and discernment needed to identify and to deal with such false prophets, whether they operate locally, nationally or internationally.

The relationship test (21-23)

In this section, Jesus teaches that some people are mistaken in thinking that they are in the Kingdom of Heaven when, in fact, they are not. He goes on to make it quite clear that members of the Kingdom are those who have a personal relationship with God.

Face the music

Jesus says: ' "Not everyone who says to me, 'Lord, Lord,' will enter the kingdom of heaven, but only he who does the will of my Father who is in heaven" ' (21). We don't enter the Kingdom by paying mere lip-service to Jesus as Lord: it's not a matter of talking obedience by just saying that Jesus is our Lord. Jesus expects to see us living lives that demonstrate such obedience by the fact that we seek to do God's will in our lives day by day. This is a part of the relationship test. If we are truly children of God, then we shall willingly obey our heavenly

Father. Such an attitude testifies to the fact that a relationship does exist between us and God.

It is important to acknowledge Jesus as Lord with our lips (Romans 10:9), but that expression of obedience must also impact our lives, changing them radically. Unfortunately, there are many people today who would claim to be Christians, and would own Jesus as Lord with their lips, but they have never repented of their sin and asked God to come into their lives. They have not been 'born again'; they have not been born spiritually into the family of God (John 3:5-7). Therefore, they have no experience of God, and no relationship with God. They know *about* God, but they don't *know* God. And God doesn't know them. In His eyes, they are still unforgiven sinners and, as such, are 'evildoers' (23b). And, one day, they will have to stand before God and face the music.

The expression 'face the music' possibly originated in Japan. The story is told of how the conductor of the imperial orchestra allowed a rich and influential man to be a part of the orchestra, so he could fulfil his desire to 'perform' before the Emperor. Even though the man couldn't read music or play an instrument, the conductor sat him in the second row of the orchestra, and gave him a flute. When a concert began, he would go through all the motions of playing the flute, without making a sound. This went on for two years; then a new conductor took over. He demanded that each instrumentalist play personally in front of him. The man with the flute tried to get out of his audition, but in the end he had to confess that he was a fake. He was unable to 'face the music'.

Those who merely go through the motions of being Christians will one day have to stand and face the music. No one will be able to hide. How we need to pray earnestly for those who are in this position, that they will come to know God for themselves, so they will never hear those awful words when they stand before God: ' "I never knew you" ' (23).

False pretences

Surprisingly, perhaps, nor do we enter into the Kingdom by means of doing great exploits in the name of Jesus. And just look at what these people had done! They had prophesied, driven out demons and performed many miracles in the name of Jesus (22). Yet Jesus describes them as 'evildoers' (23). But surely they had been doing good, not evil? So why does Jesus condemn them in this way?

This group of people were evildoers for two reasons. Although they might have done some good, they were actually doing something intrinsically evil. They were using the name of Jesus to bring glory to themselves, not to bring glory to God. They were not acting out of a relationship with God, and thus they were using His name under false pretences. Secondly, what they were doing had not impacted their lives. Indeed, their sinful lifestyles continued to deny the very Lord they claimed to be acting on behalf of. When they stand before God 'on that day' (22a), His reply to them also will be 'I never knew you' (23).

Hammer at the door

In May 1964, West Ham United, known as 'the Hammers', played Preston North End in the FA Cup Final at the old Wembley stadium. One of the West Ham players had taken a cuddly toy belonging to one of his children into the changing room for every match, and obviously felt it was bringing the team luck. Imagine his despair, then, when he got into the

Wembley changing room to find that he'd left it on the team coach! Fortunately, they were there in plenty of time; so he made his way back to the bus, and retrieved the toy.

But when he tried to get back into the ground, he found his way barred by the stewards. He pleaded with them to let him in, telling them that he was a West Ham player. Those experienced stewards told him they weren't born yesterday, and refused to let him in. He began to look round desperately for someone who knew him, but in vain. Time went on. Suddenly, he saw a face he recognised, and accompanied him to the door. Then the stewards let him in without hesitation, because he knew the referee, and the referee knew him.

'On that day', it's whom you *know* that counts.

Two Foundations (24-27)

Characteristics of 'the wise man'

Jesus begins this final section of teaching in the 'Sermon on the Mount' with the word 'Therefore'. On this occasion, though, the link is not just with a previous statement or section, but with all the teaching He has given in this great sermon.

Jesus says that, to be considered 'wise', we have to fulfil two requirements. Firstly, to hear what Jesus has been teaching us; secondly, to put these teachings into practice in our everyday lives (24a). Unfortunately, some people fail to accomplish the first one, let alone the second. They may hear the words, but they drift in through one ear and out through the other, without finding a lodging place in the mind.

On another occasion, Jesus used the sentence ' "He who has ears, let him hear" ' (Matthew 13:9). We all may have ears, but we aren't always 'all ears' to hear what God is saying to us. But, even if we do acknowledge the significance of Jesus' teachings, and admit that they merit serious consideration, unless we are prepared to move on to the next stage and actually apply them to our lives and obey them, then they remain mere words. Putting them into practice is vital, and God expects to see evidence of our doing this.

Great and greater expectations

To put it another way, God has great expectations of all those who claim to be members of His Kingdom, and He expects to see us fulfilling these expectations in our lives. In our study of the 'Sermon on the Mount', we have become aware of what some of these expectations are.

In chapter 1 we saw how the beatitudes reveal that God expects us to show the following characteristics: a recognition of our sinful state before Him; contrition for our sins; meekness, as expressed through gentle strength, humility, consideration for others, and being teachable; wanting more than anything else to live lives that are right in God's sight and to work for righteousness in society; showing mercy to those who do wrong to us; having pure hearts before God; a determination to live at peace with others and to work for reconciliation between others; being joyful, even in times of opposition or persecution.

In chapter 2 we learnt how God expects us to be actively involved in society, influencing it for the good. In chapter 3 we saw how God expects us to be obedient to His laws; to show a willingness to be reconciled to others; to exercise rigorous self-discipline in the areas of anger and lust; to uphold marriage, and take our vows very seriously; to seek restoration rather than divorce; to be truthful at all times; never to seek retaliation or revenge; to love everyone, including our enemies; and to treat others as we would like to be treated. In chapter 4 we learnt that God expects us to give to the poor, pray and fast for the right reasons, and not out of hypocritical motives; we also learned the way in which He expects us to pray, and what He expects us to include in our prayers.

In chapter 5 we saw how God expects us to be concerned about heavenly, not earthly, things, serving Him rather than chasing after money; to show trust in Him rather than to worry, and to have the right priorities; not to be judgemental, and to deal with our own faults before presuming to point out the faults of others; to be discerning as we share and teach the Gospel. In this chapter we have learnt how God expects us to pray with the right attitude; to walk His narrow way; to be on our guard against false teaching, and to be ruthless with false prophets; to acknowledge Jesus faithfully as Lord of our lives, with all that implies, and to bring glory to His name in everything we do; to put all the teachings of Jesus into practice.

God expects us to be persistent and humble in prayer; to show compassion to all in need, irrespective of their race, colour or religion; to forgive unconditionally, and to keep on forgiving; to use the gifts God has given us fully in His service; to involve ourselves in the social problems and needs of the world; to use the means at our disposal to help the poor and needy; to be ready, watching and waiting for the return of Jesus in power and glory. Great expectations indeed; and certainly far greater than those demanded by the kingdom of this world.

Before the battle of Trafalgar in 1805, Admiral Nelson signalled this message to his fleet: 'England expects every man will do his duty'. God has far greater expectations of us than Nelson had of his men. But they are ones which we should want to fulfil in our lives: not out of duty, as in the case of Nelson's sailors; but out of love. And it is as we seek to show evidence of these in our lives that we become more and more distinct from the world around us, thus enabling people to see clearly the attractive, alternative lifestyle and culture that is the Kingdom of God.

Contrasting construction and consequences

To illustrate the importance of putting His teachings into practice, Jesus tells a story which may seem at first sight to be about two houses; but it's actually about two foundations. The man Jesus describes as 'wise' built his house 'on the rock' (24b). Luke's account says that he ' "dug down deep and laid the foundation on rock" ' (Luke 6:48a). This must have taken him a great deal of time, and required much effort, persistence, endeavour, and commitment to the task. His determination to build on rock may well have meant accepting certain restrictions and constraints on the building of his house; but he was willing to make the necessary sacrifices in order to build on a secure foundation.

By contrast, the 'foolish man' built his house 'on sand'. Luke's account says that he built ' "on the ground without a foundation" ' (Luke 6:49a). This required much less effort, was much easier, and involved no restrictions or constraints whatever. When both houses were finally constructed, there appeared to be no differences between them, apart from their outward design.

But when ' "the rain came down, the streams rose, and the winds blew and beat against that house" ' (25a, 27a), there were contrasting consequences. When the storm came, attacking on all fronts, then the differences between the houses became plain for all to see. The house founded on rock 'did not fall', whereas the one built on sand 'fell with a great crash' (25b, 27b). Luke's account says of the latter: 'it collapsed and its destruction was complete' (Luke 6:49b). And it was all down, literally, to the foundations.

Violent storms, which Denis Baly describes as being of 'concentrated fury', were commonplace in Palestine from November onwards; so Jesus' hearers would have known from personal experience exactly what He was talking about.

Foolishness

Nobody in real life would be foolish enough to build his house on anything other than firm and deep foundations. Jesus is saying how foolish it is of people not to build their lives on the solid foundation of His teaching. Many who listened to Jesus agreed with His teachings, but were not putting them into practice. They were just paying lip-service to Him. This was still happening in the early church (James 1:22). The true disciples were those who both listened to and obeyed His teachings in their lives. When the storms came, their faith would stand like a house built on rock. No matter what crisis, trouble or persecution came, their faith and trust in God would never waver. The opposite would be true of those who paid only lip-service to Jesus. Indeed, the storms of persecution soon descended upon the followers of Jesus, clearly distinguishing those who were true disciples from those who wavered and 'collapsed' in the face of this fierce onslaught.

There are also those today who claim to be Christians, and yet their faith is very shallow. They have not 'dug down deep'. They are 'hearers' of the word, but not 'doers'. Jesus' teaching is not the basis of their lives, and so when they are beset by problems and difficulties from all sides, they have nothing to draw guidance or strength from. The tragic result is that their faith often collapses under the strain and stress caused by the storms. This is not to say that those whose lives are founded deep in the teachings of Jesus, and are characterised by obedience, don't get battered by the storms of life. Not at all. But what it does mean is that they are able to stand secure through times of trouble, because of the depth of their foundations in the rock, Christ Jesus.

It seems to me that when Jesus talks about those who are foolish in respect of their lives' foundations, He is not just talking about those who claim to be His disciples. True, the word 'Therefore' at the start of this section (24) does link what He goes on to say with the teachings that have gone before. However, when He uses the phrase 'these words of mine' (24a, 26a), He would surely have been including all the teachings that He gave, not just those that would be contained in this sermon. In other words, the message of the Gospel in all its fullness.

This brings another possible meaning into play. The 'foolish' are now all those who reject the Gospel message. Some prefer to build their lives on the teaching of philosophers, or those they regard as prophets. Others choose the shifting sands of ever-changing social and moral values, where there are no absolutes, no certainties, and therefore no lasting security. The attractiveness of this latter choice is that there are no restrictions or constraints, as there are when building on the rock; although the restraints given are purely for our own good. Nevertheless, as sinful human beings, we do not welcome building regulations in our lives, even if they come from a divine and loving architect-designer! Eventually, houses built on questionable or no particular foundations are bound to crash in the face of the storms which come into the lives of all of us.

A broken brick

When workmen began to renovate the Theatre London in London, Ontario, they were determined to save the theatre's greatest glory: its splendid proscenium arch with its hand-painted murals of frolicking nymphs. During the project's early stages, they discovered that one side of the arch was supported by nothing more than a broken brick standing on loose sand. A steel support was hastily erected before the arch collapsed!

Are we building our lives on nothing more than broken bricks standing on loose sand? Or could Jesus describe us as being wise builders, who fulfil both His requirements: builders known to Him for our effort, persistence, endeavour and commitment to the task of being His disciples; builders who are so determined to build on the rock that we willingly accept the restrictions, restraints and sacrifices required in order to live according to His teachings?

Ultimate authority

Matthew tells us that 'When Jesus had finished saying these things, the crowds were amazed at his teaching' (28). And the reason for their amazement was not just the content of what He said, but 'because he taught as one who had authority, and not as their teachers of the law' (29). Mark records an identical reaction to His teaching in the synagogue at Capernaum: 'The people were amazed at his teaching, because he taught them as one who had authority, not as the teachers of the law' (Mark 1:22).

They were used to going along to the synagogue week after

week and hearing the rabbis arguing over the finer points of what the Law said. If a person asked them a question about the Law, they would usually quote a particular teaching, and back up what they had said by referring to what some other rabbi had stated in the past; a bit like lawyers do today. They did this to give their words more authority. 'Quibbling and quoting' is how Eugene Peterson in The Message describes what went on.

Jesus, on the other hand, never did this. He didn't spend His time arguing about nuances of meaning that were over the heads of most of the people. Nor did He quote what other teachers of the Law had said when He was asked a question. His authority was not based on support from other rabbis. He was teaching them new things, and was teaching them with an authority that stemmed from God, from Christ Himself, not from rabbis whom He could quote.

Jesus is the ultimate authority because He *is* God (John 10:30). He spoke with divine authority, unlike all the other religious teachers, none of whom ever claimed to be God. It seems to me that this fact has two major implications. Firstly, that we must resist with vigour all attempts to downgrade the teachings of Jesus to the level of those given by other teachers. Secondly, that it behoves all of us who claim to be disciples of Christ to make it our business to know what He said, and, by His grace and power, to live lives which fulfil these greater expectations.

Questions for group study

Matthew 7:7-29

Verses 7-11

Discuss

1 In what three ways does Jesus teach that we are to be persistent in prayer?

Apply

2 Why do we often find it difficult to be persistent in our praying?
3 What encouragement can we take from the word 'will' (7)?
4 Why is it that answers to our prayers do not usually come immediately?

Discuss

5 Some people think verses 7-9 mean that God will grant us anything we ask for. Do we agree with this?
6 What point is Jesus making by comparing the response of an earthly father and our heavenly Father to a request made by one of their children (9-11)?

Apply

7. Is whether we pray regularly or not a good indicator of the current state of our relationship with God?

[Note: verse 12 is covered in chapter 3.]

Verses 13, 14

Discuss

8 Why does Jesus urge us to choose the 'narrow' road?

Apply

9 What expectations does choosing this road bring?

Discuss

10 Why is the gate to this road also described as 'narrow'?

Apply

11 What implications does this have for living and witnessing in a multi-faith society where all roads are said to lead to God?

Discuss

12 Why is the other road described by Jesus as being 'broad'?

13 Why is the gate to it described as 'wide'?

Apply

14 Why is a life lived walking the narrow road and obeying God's laws the best choice?

Discuss

15 How is the statement that 'only a few find it' applicable today?

Apply

16 What challenges does this present to us?

Verses 15-20

Background
17 What does the New Testament have to say on the subject of false prophets?

Discuss
18 Why does Jesus describe such people as wolves in sheep's clothing?

Apply
19 How can we in our church make sure that we are not deceived?

20 What experiences have group members had of such people in the past?

Discuss
21 Why did Jesus tell us to apply the 'fruit test'?

Apply
22 What can we learn from what happened in the churches at Ephesus, Pergamum and Thyatira (Revelation 2:2b, 6; 2:14-16; 2:20a)?

23 In what two particular areas do we need to apply the fruit test rigorously?

24 In this regard, what can we learn from the following references: Luke 6:45; 1 John 2:22; 2 John verses 7-9; 2 Timothy 2:16-18; Titus 1:9-11?

Discuss
25 In spite of the warnings of Scripture, why are many Christians still deceived?

Verses 21-23
Discuss
26 Why is the relationship test critical?

Apply
27 What is the evidence in our lives of a relationship with God?

28 How can we persuade people who consider themselves Christians of the need to be 'born again'?

Discuss
29 How can people who have prophesied, driven out demons and performed miracles in the name of Jesus be described as 'evildoers'?

Apply
30 What warning does this give us?

Verses 24-27
Discuss
31 What are the two requirements we need to fulfil in order to be considered 'wise' in God's sight?

Apply
32 What is the difference between the sailors fulfilling

Nelson's expectations, and our fulfilling God's greater expectations?
33 What will be the result of our seeking to fulfil His expectations?

Imagine
34 Brainstorm words to describe the qualities shown by the man who built his house on the rock.

Discuss
35 Who are represented by the foolish man?
36 What did the storm reveal?

Background
37 What did the storm represent in the lives of those who heard Jesus' teachings?
38 What effect did it have on them?

Apply
39 Why is it essential that our lives are founded deep in the teachings of Jesus?

Discuss
40 Who could the foolish man also represent?
41 On what sort of foundations do people build their lives?

Apply
42 What are the requirements that 'wise' builders fulfil?
43 Would Jesus describe us as 'wise'?

Verses 28, 29
Discuss
44 Why were the crowds amazed at Jesus' teaching?

Apply
45 Why is it significant for us that Jesus spoke with divine authority?

For personal prayer and reflection

Am I persistent in prayer?
Am I guilty of treating God like a celestial vending machine?
Is prayer a fundamental part of my relationship with God?
Having chosen to walk the narrow road, am I living my life accordingly?
Do others see something different and appealing in my lifestyle which will challenge them about theirs?
Do I test everything I hear against what the Bible says, or am I too easily influenced by the person speaking?
Do I willingly obey my heavenly Father, or just pay lip-service to His commands?
Do I know God, and does He know me?
Do I always seek to glorify God and not myself in everything I do?
When the storms come into my life, how do I fare?
Would Jesus describe me as 'wise'?